4 . 2 . 81

Religious education and religious understanding

Religious education and religious understanding

An introduction to the philosophy of religious education

Raymond Holley

Senior Lecturer in Religious Studies
West London Institute of Higher Education

Routledge & Kegan Paul
London, Henley and Boston

First published in 1978
by Routledge & Kegan Paul Ltd
39 Store Street,
London WC1E 7DD,
Broadway House,
Newtown Road,
Henley-on-Thames,
Oxon RG9 1EN and
9 Park Street,
Boston, Mass. 02108, USA
Phototypeset in V.I.P. Bembo by
Western Printing Services Ltd, Bristol
and printed in Great Britain by
Redwood Burn Ltd
Trowbridge and Esher
© Raymond Holley 1978

British Library Cataloguing in Publication Data

Holley, Raymond
  Religious education and religious understanding.
  1. Religious education – Philosophy
  I. Title
  200'.7   BV1464   78–40590

  ISBN 7100 8995 3

In memory of my father
Sidney Edward Frank Holley
10 May 1899–26 February 1976
'See you in the summer'

He seems to me a very foolish man and very wretched
who will not increase his understanding while he is in the
world, and ever wish and long to reach that endless life
where all shall be made clear.

King Alfred the Great

O the mind, mind has mountains; cliffs of fall
Frightful, sheer, no-man-fathomed. Hold them cheap
May who ne'er hung there. Nor does long our small
Durance deal with that steep or deep. Here! creep,
Wretch under a comfort serves in a whirlwind: all
Life death does end and each day dies with sleep

Gerard Manley Hopkins

Press on, my mind! Go forward with all your strength!
God is our hope. He made us and not we ourselves. Go
forward toward the place where truth begins to dawn.

St Augustine

Contents

Contents

Preface

This little book about religious education is avowedly philosophical in genre but it is not intended to be a work in the field of pure philosophy or in that of philosophy of religion. Instead it is offered as an introduction to the philosophy of religious education.

During the last fifteen years there has been published a variety of books dealing with every imaginable aspect of religious education. Reports on the state of the subject, advice on methods, psychological studies of children's religious thinking, outlines for assemblies, proposals for examinations, sociological studies of particular groups of children studying religion and observations on the relations between religious education and moral education have all been offered to the interested reader. The national newspapers have not been slow in reporting the activities of various 'pressure groups' or in taking opportunities to voice 'opinions'.

Implicit in all these efforts are various presuppositions about religious education, both logical and factual. It is the task of philosophy of religious education to make explicit the logical presuppositions of the enterprise, to trace their interdependence and entailments and, where possible, to suggest what inferences might be drawn for the practice of teaching religion in an educational way.

In some ways this task is still in its infancy. Articles in the field have appeared in educational journals but the amount of literature is minimal compared with that, for example, in psychological studies related to religious education. Accordingly this introduction does not attempt to 'view the field', as it were, and to present summaries of various viewpoints. It is not intended as a 'reader'. Instead it attempts to put forward a particular theory of religious education in such a way as to embrace major questions and at the same time to encourage readers to do some philosophy of religious education by disagreeing with the author.

I have been aided by a good many people in writing this book, not least my students. H. W. Marratt was the first to give me the opportunity to lecture in philosophy of religious education and, for the past eight years, my colleagues W. N. Greenwood and D. A. Lawes have encouraged me in all manner of ways to press on with my writing. Of my teachers Miss J. M. Cooper supervised the preparation of my thesis for the degree of MPhil and Professor R. S. Peters has guided me patiently and wisely through many sloughs of despond. And my wife and daughters have sacrificed much in order that this might be written. I am grateful to them all. I only ask the reader not to impute to any of them responsibility for the arguments paraded here. I alone accept responsibility for them.

I am grateful to the Christian Education Movement, as publishers of the journal *Learning for Living*, for permission to incorporate in chapters 1 and 6 some of the material which was originally published in articles in that journal in March 1971 and March 1975.

Chapter 1

Aims of religious education

He who has an aim has a law over him; he does not merely guide himself; he is guided. An aim sets limits; but limits are the mentors of virtue.

L. Feuerbach: *The Essence of Christianity*

Introduction

There is a story of a young man who was setting out upon a medical career. His long and expensive training had been financed largely by a maiden aunt and, being a grateful and dutiful nephew, he often visited her to report on his progress. On one occasion he laid out for her his plans for life – house surgeon, marriage, specialism leading to consultancy and then early retirement in order to enjoy himself after years of hard work. 'And what then?' inquired his aunt. 'Death, presumably', replied the nephew with a wry chuckle. 'And then?' persisted his aunt. 'How should I know!' exclaimed the young man. 'You may not know', his aunt rejoined, 'but you ought to be thinking about it.'

One can imagine the young doctor being both slightly amused and surprised at his aunt's interest in such long-term intentions and possibilities but on reflection he might have appreciated a fundamental truth about life underlying the old lady's remarks. It is that much of what we do voluntarily, together with the way in which we do it, is largely determined by the goals we set ourselves. If we set our sights on being a

1

millionaire by the time we are thirty years old, or on achieving a PhD before we marry, or on having five children after we are married then we shall live our lives accordingly.

This truth about life – that our intentions and goals shape our freely determined life-style – not only pertains to the more grandiose schemes we devise but also to the thousand-and-one activities which make up daily life. Thus, in order to characterize and categorize the different activities in which people engage we often refer to the end, or goal, or intention which is envisaged. 'What are you doing?' one asks a neighbour so obviously mixing concrete: and the import of the question is, 'What is your intention? To lay a garden path?' Or one walks indoors and finds it impossible to get into the lounge because the floor, chairs, couch and tables are covered with pieces of paper, material, pins and needles, and reels of cotton. 'Oh,' says your mother, 'your sister's making a dress.'

To put the matter succinctly, activities are inherently teleological. When a state of affairs is described as an 'activity' there is both an end in mind (hence 'teleological' from the Greek *telos* meaning 'end' or 'completion') and the particular end, or ends, largely affects the content and procedures within the activity. So if one wishes to build a garage to house as expensive and inflammable a thing as a motor car (if that is the *telos* of your activity) there is far more sense in using bricks and mortar than piles of old newspapers. Being clear about what one intends to achieve in an activity is of no small importance because the intention will largely determine the very steps taken in the procedures which make up the activity.

1 The practical importance of aims in RE

This underlining of the importance of intentions in activities is highly pertinent in religious education for sheltering under that overall title is a host of diverse activities. Many of these activities are teaching activities and nowadays there is great stress laid upon studying methods of teaching religion. Indeed, it is sometimes argued that one begins with a study of methods rather than with the academic content of religious education because what is to be taught will depend very much upon the ways in which one is prepared to teach. And there is some validity and truth in such an approach: there *is* a very close association between what is to be taught and the ways in which we are prepared to teach children.

The choice of content and method cannot be decided, however, until questions about the goals the teacher intends to achieve have been settled. 'Drama' may be a useful method of teaching religion with, say, eleven-year-old children: and the life of Elijah might be taught through drama. But however attractive such ideas might be they must be jettisoned if they do not accord with the objectives one has in mind for those particular children in religious education. What one hopes to *achieve* in religious education is of prime importance, not methods or content. Only when this has been settled do the questions about procedure become manageable. And this is not a matter of tradition – of dyed-in-the-wool practitioners refusing to clamber out of their comfortable ruts in order to face new challenges – but of plain logic.

Talk about goals, ends, targets, achievements and intentions of activities is logically prior to talk about the procedures and content of the activities. This means that one has to get clear about one's aims and intentions in any activity before one can be clear about how such ends are to be achieved. Hence all the talk about 'aims of religious education' and the emphasis laid upon their importance.

Such talk about aims of religious education is very much of practical importance because the choice of aims by the teacher will largely determine the kind of religious education his pupils receive. A teacher might choose to set out to achieve particular goals which would result in the children receiving very little, if any, genuine religious education at all simply because the aims which gave direction to his work were not in accord with the whole notion of 'religious education'. So the questions which arise about aims of religious education are not simply descriptive, i.e. 'What *are* the aims of religious education?' but also evaluative, i.e. 'What *ought* to be the aims of religious education?'

Unfortunately these two kinds of question are sometimes run together and different aims which are in fact being pursued in certain schools are paraded as desirable. But just because a practice exists, or is recommended, or is even required by

3

those in authority does not of itself make that practice either coherent or desirable. Indeed some aims which are pursued under the banner of 'religious education' ought not to be striven after because they are not religiously educational. Accordingly the questions about what ought to be the aims in this area are of similar importance to the practising teacher as are those about existing aims. It is the purpose of this chapter to begin to tussle with such questions but before clear answers can be given it is necessary to note some peculiarities about 'aims of religious education' both in terms of what could, and could not, be meant by such talk and about the way in which different kinds of aim function both independently and inter-dependently.

2   Meaningful talk about aims

The initial difficulty in any talk about 'aims' and 'religious education' is that one becomes so used to hearing such talk that its peculiarities are not noticed: and this can lead to slipshod thinking which in turn engenders bad educational practice. In ordinary speech the notions of 'aim' on the one hand, and 'religion' and 'education' on the other hand, are inappropriate bedfellows because 'aim' usually implies some external target and neither 'education' nor 'religion' has such targets.

The ball of scrap paper is aimed at the waste-paper basket: the dart is aimed at the board in the public bar: the goal-seeking footballer takes aim before unleashing a shot. Whenever the verb 'to aim' is used the implicit meaning is that of arriving at an achievement which, whilst determining the procedures and processes leading up to it, is in a sense apart from these actions. On looking for a fox in a covert one achieves one's aim when the animal is seen running into an adjacent field of kale. But whilst the 'looking for' has the target of 'seeing' the fox the two are obviously not the same. One could look for a fox without success: and one could see a fox quite by accident when walking along a road. Talk about aims of procedures and activities often implies a goal to be achieved at the end, a possible rounding-off and completion which is not to be equated with, and identified with, the processes themselves which lead up to it. It is because of this that there is a certain sense of failure if the goal is not reached. The path is *not* the prize.

With this in mind it can now be seen that to talk of 'aims of (religious) education' *might* be to imply that there are goals to be achieved through educational processes which are somewhat different from those processes themselves. Some people do mean just this when, for example, they postulate the production of 'good citizens' or 'well-integrated persons' or even 'critical TV-viewers' as the goal of eleven years of education. But however noble and pleasant an idea may seem, or however sweetly it is voiced, this of itself does not make the idea reasonable or sensible. And the reason why any reference to 'aims of education' is misleading when it means 'targets external to and reached through education' is that 'education' is not the name of any particular processes and activities and therefore cannot have any such aims of its own. Training, drilling, schooling, conditioning and indoctrinating may all have such 'external' aims: but education cannot.

'Education' does not *describe* any action in detail: instead it is a kind of accolade one awards to certain actions and activities which meet particular standards. It is a notion which functions in a similar way to 'friendly'. Some actions and intentions are, we say, friendly: others are not. And in so saying we are evaluating the actions and activities according to standards built into our notions of 'friendliness' or 'friendship'. Because of this it is said that notions like 'education' and 'friendly' are evaluative concepts: they do not name and describe processes and activities but select from amongst them.

If a crude scientific analogy will be permitted, evaluative concepts are like litmus paper dipped into liquids in order to select and differentiate: only the 'liquids' are activities, processes and procedures like writing essays, playing games, acquiring knowledge and learning skills. These activities may have aims: and the aims may be educational. But 'education' cannot have aims, any more than 'friendship' can have an external target. Indeed one way of casting doubt upon the sincerity of a person's friendliness is to question his intention in a purportedly 'friendly' act. 'Friendly' acts which have an external aim (e.g. promotion, or the selfish accruing of money) are hardly to be categorized as 'friendship'. If friendship can ever be said to have any aim at all it is that of friendship itself: and the same can be said of education. It cannot have an external target even though there be some worthwhile spin-off. But to pursue it solely for instrumental purposes is not to pursue it at all.[1]

There are similar peculiarities in talking about 'aims of religion'. Taking Christianity as an example of one particular religion, the idea that faith in God can be thought to have an aim will appear ridiculous to the Christian. To be 'religious' in the Christian sense in order to achieve some further objective (social standing?) is not simply to be misguided but irreligious. And any action or activity undertaken because of that faith, or as an expression of the believer's trust in God, whilst it will have its own aim (e.g. to relieve suffering), will nevertheless not constitute the whole of the Christian life and will be termed 'Christian' only inasmuch as it corresponds to the standards and beliefs of the Faith. Even though a whole life of activity and involvement be said to be done *ad gloriam Dei* this must not be understood as implying that there is some separate objective (perhaps hereafter) apart from the living of the life of faith. It is in the actual living of the Christian life, in the actual doing of Christian actions that God is glorified. There is no product separate from the life which praises God. In the religious (Christian) life the path *is* the prize.

To speak about the 'aims of religious education' is misguided and unintelligent if what is implied is that there is some objective(s) external to religious education, and different from being religiously educated, which can be and ought to be achieved through it. Whenever one states educational aims one 'will be drawing attention not to some terminating point to education or to life, but to values intrinsic to the quality of life which being educated makes possible'.[2]

Those activities on the part of teachers and pupils which constitute religious education in a task sense are those concerned with the pupils being religiously educated. And talk about 'aims in religious education' is talk about aims of activities which are religiously educational. This entails reference to those values implicit in the notion of 'religious education' which should determine the choice of activities undertaken whereby the children do have a chance of being religiously educated persons.

In facing the question, 'What ought to be the aims of religious education?' it may be best understood as meaning, 'Which are those activities whose aims best meet the values implicit in the notion of religious education?', or, 'What steps need to be taken for a child to be a religiously educated person?' The one thing it cannot mean is, 'What are the legitimate external targets to be achieved through religious education?' or, 'What kind of people do we wish to produce through religious education (other than being religiously educated)?' As a series of tasks and activities religious education must not be reduced to some form of social engineering.

3   The functions of aims

The practical significance of understanding aims of religious education as being aims of activities and processes and procedures according with standards implicit in 'religious education' is not to be gainsaid. In the first place such talk focuses attention upon those activities which are desirable, worthwhile and necessary in religious education. The teacher in the classroom has a hundred-and-one things to do every day. The children are to be welcomed, the register marked, the windows opened and care taken to make sure that the children are comfortable (and not sitting in wet clothes) before any subject teaching can even begin. And when one does begin to teach there are often numerous tasks to be undertaken simply to do with physical organization of the class and classroom. It is all too easy for a teacher to get bogged down in the minutiae of everyday affairs – many of them of a purely bureaucratic nature – and to lose sight of genuine educational activities. Intelligent and meaningful talk about 'aims in (religious) education' helps to focus the mind upon what is really important in the classroom, and in the wider life of the school, and thereby may motivate the teacher to cut through the relatively unimportant as quickly as possible and get down to necessary and essential work.

A second problem for the teacher (often stemming from the first) is that it is altogether too easy to lose sight of the overall educational career of the children: to concentrate so much upon the lesson or scheme in hand that one forgets both the pupils' past and their potential future. This is only to be expected for one cannot be thinking of all this at the same time as one is concentrating on something as mundane and yet important as ensuring that, say, ten-year-old children can spell correctly such key words as 'Jesus', 'altar' or 'Maundy Thursday'. Being able to summarize both past achievements and future possibilities both succinctly and comprehensively therefore becomes important, and in this matter what some might call 'long-term' aims in (religious) education are useful vehicles. They can sum up what has been achieved and what it is hoped will be achieved, for aims are always statements of practicable direction.

As statements of practicable direction those aims which do accord with the values implicit in the notion of 'religious education' help to overcome what might on occasions be a quite serious matter – *viz*. the sheer diversity of academic content, methods and approaches possible in the teaching of any matter to any children, which can lead to some children being educationally underprivileged. Some countries try to overcome this problem by insisting on a strict national timetable whereby all the children in the country of a particular age-group learn the same matter at the same time (and often, one suspects, in a stereotyped manner). But this seems to be a case of employing sledgehammers to crack nuts.

There is no one method which can be said to be *the* right method of teaching a particular matter to particular children, although some methods will seem more appropriate than others. And there is not always a necessary connection between academic material and a particular educational objective (witness the thousands of saints whose biographies could be employed to teach primary school children about the power and graciousness of God the Holy Spirit). Furthermore, individual teachers and children have different interests and possess different knowledge. So there is always the possibility of great diversity of 'teachings' going on in the same large school, and certainly amongst different schools. But this does not matter as long as the religious education given is genuinely 'religious' and genuinely 'educative' and one way of ensuring this is to gain agreement on what ought to be the aims in religious education so that there is coherence of the numerous enterprises.

Aims in religious education, then, have great practical importance in focusing attention upon what is of fundamental importance amongst the numerous activities going on in the classroom, of succinctly summarizing years of work and study, and of providing cohesive direction to numerous distinct enterprises. But this having been said a proviso must be added immediately. It is that there are at least three different jobs which 'aims' are said to be doing here: and this means either that aims in religious education are highly flexible or that there are different kinds of aim which function in different ways.

If it is the case that the aims are highly flexible then they must all be stated in general, though not vague, terms otherwise they cannot be flexible. An example of this might be, 'to enable the children to achieve religious insights through the study of religious literature'. The problem with this kind of statement of practicable direction is that whilst it is flexible and practical, and does give direction to one's work it is nevertheless too general to be employed as an aim of a specific activity limited by considerations of time and children's ability. It could never be acceptable for one lesson because as such it is thoroughly impracticable: one could never cover sufficient ground in one lesson with children of any age to have any hope whatsoever of getting close to achieving such an aim. The alternative seems to be the case: that there are different kinds of aim in religious education which function in different ways, which do different jobs.

4 Four kinds of aim

Of the different kinds of aim in religious education there seem to be four in number and I shall call them (i) the general aim, (ii) the stage aim, (iii) the scheme aim, and (iv) the lesson aim. There might be some argument as to whether in fact there are other kinds as well but bearing in mind a philosophical principle laid down centuries ago by William of Ockham, that one should not multiply classes and categories unnecessarily, it can usually be shown that these four categories suffice. What needs to be done now is to get clear about what is meant by these titles, about the interrelatedness of the aims, about their differences in function and, finally, the practical significance of all this in attempting to answer the question, 'What ought to be the aims in religious education?'

(i) *General aims*   By a 'general aim' is meant a formal, general statement covering all religiously educational activities indulged in throughout the child's career at school. As such it is not the goal, target or intention of any particular activity, or particular group of activities, but rather expresses and indicates the kind of approach and line of general direction to be adopted by all teachers of religious education. As such it is much more a statement of policy than a detailed directive, a strategic plan than a list of orders. An example of such is:[3]

> The aim of religious education [is] the promotion of understanding. It uses the tools of scholarship in order to enter into an empathic experience of the faith of individuals and groups. It does not seek to promote any one religious viewpoint but it recognizes that the study of religion must transcend the merely informative.

(ii) *Stage aims*   The 'stage aims' are those appertaining to the various stages of thinking through which both commonsense observations and studies in child psychology tell us all children progress. The infant is so obviously different from the sixth-former in interests and abilities that it would be unwise in the extreme to have identical aims in religious education for both – 'identical', that is, in terms of learning content and possible insights. Examples of stage aims are:[4]

> *4–7 years old*: One of its [RE's] aims is to create a community where children know they are loved, where they can feel confident and secure, and where they share together in the adventure of growing up. [RE] should aim at the enriching of children's general experience and the strengthening of their community life.

> *11–18 years old*: the essential aim underlying the themes is the enrichment of the experience of young people by help-

ing them to appreciate the significance of Jesus Christ, especially as they establish their own values, attitudes and philosophy of life.

(iii) *Scheme aims*   It has long been found desirable for purposes of efficiency to pursue a number of schemes of work during a school term or year. Such a scheme usually is evolved from, and revolves around, a topic or theme but the work and study can be haphazard and disjointed unless it has a clear objective which can be achieved in the time available. Scheme aims tend to summarize a particular unit of learning to be mastered through a series of related and interrelated activities and procedures.

(iv) *Lesson aims*   Finally the lesson aim is severe in its particularity, very limited and highly precise, making specific reference to learning content. Often it is the goal of only a single activity. By calling such an aim a 'lesson aim' it must not be construed that there is some surreptitious argument here to the effect that religious education can only be pursued in traditional 'set' lessons, or that religiously educational activities cannot be integrated with other subjects or be part of a project. The intention is to draw attention to the kind of aim with which the experienced teacher is so familiar and which the student-teacher so often finds difficult to grasp and formulate, *viz*. the very precise yet limited intention which needs to be realized time and time again if there is to be any teaching in depth as well as breadth.

(v) *The interrelatedness of the aims*   Whilst these four kinds of aim are distinct they are also interrelated. One way of thinking of this relationship is in terms of different levels of dependence of the one upon the other. As the general aim indicates the approach to be adopted in religiously educational activities, rather than specific learning content, so it cannot operate alone without the lesson aim. On the other hand, the lesson aim itself is altogether too limited to give viable scope and coherence to the ongoing processes in religious education: it needs to be understood and justified in the light of the scheme, stage and general aims. 'To ensure that the children know the chrono-

11

logy of the events of Holy Week' may be a thoroughly worthy lesson aim – but only if it is a relevant part of a larger scheme or syllabus of work which is concerned with the provocation of broader and deeper understanding than is expressible simply in lists of dates and events.

5   Justifying aims

(i) *General aims*   Whilst bearing in mind interrelationships such as these one must not lose sight of the fact that any attempt to justify particular aims in religious education must take account of the kind of aim in question because the different aims function in different ways and have different though equally important parts to play.

Inasmuch as the general aims express and summarize overall approaches and attitudes to the work of religious education in all schools at all ages so they are shown to be acceptable, or otherwise, predominantly by reference to the meaning of 'religious education', or, to what it means to be religiously educated. 'To persuade children to follow in the faith of their fathers' is rejected as a general aim because it smacks of religious induction rather than education. And 'to enable the children to understand the Christian Faith' may prove unacceptable as the only, single general aim of religious education inasmuch as it is too narrow, for 'religion' as a generic term always implies more than just the Christian Faith.

The general aims make explicit in practical terms the values implicit in the notion of 'religious education': and the acceptability and desirability of a general aim lies in the reasoned demonstration of its recommendations according with the standards implied by the notion of 'religious education'. This is because it is the function of the general aim to state clearly, though in general terms, the kind of direction in which procedures and activities should progress and the kind of attitudes and approaches a teacher should adopt in his work if in fact it is to be religiously educational.

(ii) *Stage aims*   'What ought to be the general aims in religious education?' is answered then by reference to what is

meant by 'religious education' and by 'being religiously educated'. But this is by no means the case with stage aims for
these function in a different way from general aims. Stage aims
attempt to give direction in terms both of what is genuinely
religious educational and in terms of the kind of learning it is
appropriate to expect children of a particular mental age to
master. Accordingly they must reflect both philosophical
understanding of what is meant by religious education and
psychological understanding of the child and his mental
development. And it is because of the latter feature that stage
aims have been subject to the closest scrutiny over the past few
years with the growth of interest in psychological studies of
the development of religious thinking of children.

Establishing the desirability of particular stage aims is a
complex matter. In the first place one has to decide which
theory of child development is most cogent and relevant.
Secondly a distinction has to be drawn between the descriptive
accounts given by the psychologists of how the mind works
and develops and the practical recommendations which are
inferred from such descriptions. To take but one example:
given that children are incapable of mastering and employing
abstract concepts such as 'God' and 'Holy Trinity' before the
mental age of eleven years old (i.e. the description of how the
mind works) does it automatically follow from this, as a
practical recommendation, that one should not mention such
matters before the children reach that age? And having settled
these psychological matters there is still the philosophical
referent to be considered – *viz.* the meaning of 'religious
education'. So questions about what ought to be the stage aims
in religious education can only be answered by reference both
to the logic of religious education as expressed in the general
aims and to the practical inferences from findings in child
psychology.

(iii) *Scheme aims* There is a sense in which stage aims in
religious education are 'universal': that is, the ways of thinking
which can be expected of children at similar stages in their
mental development is the same for children in Gateshead as it
is for their peers in Dover and Penzance (or, even in Singapore
and Washington, if the psychologists are correct). But at any

13

one stage there is such a vast mass of potential learning content available that selection from amongst it and by each school is absolutely necessary. Hence the importance of each school having its own syllabus of religious education. This selection will necessarily be made in the light of the interests and abilities of the children, the environment of the school and the knowledge and skills of the teacher – for to ignore these in any teaching situation (educational or otherwise) is to court disaster.

For reasons of efficiency of learning the syllabus will be divided into different schemes or courses and each one of these should have an aim. The purpose of these scheme aims is to make more explicit and manageable a particular unit of learning relevant to the children's stage of development, and to give coherence and direction to numerous activities and procedures which will be encompassed by the scheme or course. A scheme aim functions both as a selector and a director and both these tasks are important when there is so much material which might be learned and so many activities over a period of some weeks in which both class and teacher may lose their way. The topic might be 'David': and one could construct a scheme of work around such a topic. But content and direction of the work will depend not only upon the biblical and extra-biblical material available but also upon the particular scheme aim selected. 'To help the children understand the religious personality of David' is a different objective from 'To help the children understand the symbolic importance of David in contemporary Judaism.' The same topic can be unfolded in quite different schemes of work: and selection of the material and the direction of the learning is necessarily dependent upon the aim chosen for the scheme.

'Which are the scheme aims which should be chosen?' is the question then. Or, 'How is the selection of particular scheme aims to be justified?' It has already been argued that determining what ought to be the stage aims in religious education is a different matter from deciding which general aims are acceptable and desirable, and the same is true of scheme aims. Their function is to select and give direction to specific units of learning for particular children in particular schools. In other words, unless such aims are relevant to (a) the mass of learning content which children at a particular stage can master, and (b) the particular abilities, aptitudes and knowledge of the children who are to do the learning, and (c) the knowledge and skills of the teachers responsible for the work, then they cannot function as scheme aims.

Table 1.1 *Functions of the different aims in religious education*

Kind of aim	Function of aim	
General	(i) to make explicit in stipulative terms of practicable direction the values implicit in the notion of 'religious education'	
	(ii) to indicate the kind of approach to, and general direction of, all religious studies in all schools	
Stage	(i) to indicate the particular learning content appropriate to the children's stage of mental development	to focus attention upon, and to give practicable direction to, what is of fundamental educational importance in the pursuits, procedures and activities going on in the school and classroom
	(ii) to provide cohesive direction to studies undertaken in different schools	
Scheme	(i) to indicate units of learning selected from the mass of learning content available at any one stage of mental development	
	(ii) to indicate a particular learning content to be mastered through a limited course of study	
	(iii) to provide cohesive direction to studies undertaken in the same school	
	(iv) to provide succinct summaries of past and future periods of study	
Lesson	to indicate a precise, specific, limited learning content to be mastered in limited time	

It is by reference to the logic of religious education as expressed in general and stage aims, and by reference also to the particular children and teachers themselves, that scheme aims are either justified or rejected. Because of these latter referents – the children and teachers – scheme aims are much less effective in providing cohesive direction to diverse activities in religious education *between* schools. Such cohesive direction is provided by the general and stage aims. But within a particular large school where more than one teacher may be responsible for the religious education of the children the scheme aims may act as cohering agents.

(iv) *Lesson aims*   Finally in determining what ought to be the lesson aims in religious education, or in deciding whether a particular lesson aim is religiously educational or not, reference must be made to the general, stage and scheme aims already decided upon – especially the relevant scheme aim. The task of the lesson aim is to make clear the precise learning content which it is intended the children shall master in the limited time available – limited both by the nature of the school organization and, more important, by the capabilities of the children to concentrate upon and attend to one coherent matter at a time.

It is because of this time factor, as well as the desirability of building up wider understanding of any matter through the acquisition of a clear grasp of smaller constituent parts, that lesson aims are so fiercely specific in nature. 'To assist twelve-year-old children to understand the life of Gotama Buddha' is much too vast ever to count as a lesson aim. It would need to be cut down to something like, 'To assist the children to know the chronology of the major events in Gotama's life' – and even then one would have to choose only a few events as 'the major events'. A good lesson aim is always highly particular. And its justification as worth while must therefore be in terms of reference to scheme aims.

(v) *The hierarchy of justification*   In facing the question, 'What ought to be the aims in religious education?' it can now be seen that before such a question can be answered it is necessary to know what kind of aim is being spoken of. The four kinds of aim are each different in function and whilst all of them give practicable direction to efforts evaluated as 'religious education' they cannot all be justified in one sweeping, monolithic way. This is not to imply that they are not interrelated and interdependent: they are. But they do function in different ways: they do operate with a logical distinctiveness. Figure 1.1 may help to make this point more clearly.

Each kind of aim has a distinct function and because of this each must be justified in a different way. Yet none of them can stand on its own, by itself. It is dependent upon the others in terms of practical application. The general aim requires the greater specificity of the scheme and lesson aims to give it purchase and direct influence upon the classroom situation: and the lesson aim must always be achieved in an atmosphere

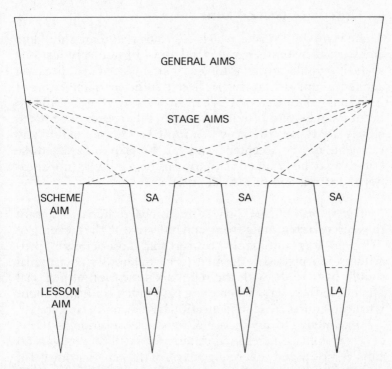

Figure 1.1 *The distinctiveness yet interdependence of different kinds of aim*

dominated by the approaches indicated by the general aims and the stage aims. Scheme aims can summarize past work and postulate future endeavours whilst providing coherence of efforts within a school, whilst general aims and stage aims have a greater cohesive value *vis-à-vis* the work in different schools. But in all of this there is a certain hierarchy of justification inasmuch as if the lesson, scheme and stage aims are to be genuine aims in religious education then they must accord with the general aims. So the question, 'What ought to be the aims in religious education?' always implies some covert reference to the general aims. It is therefore necessary to end this chapter by indicating the kind of criteria necessary for determining the desirability and acceptability of particular statements put forward as general aims in religious education.

6 Criteria of general aims

There is no golden rule which demands that there should be any particular number of general aims. Presumably just one such aim would suffice as long as it emphasized that direction and those approaches which reflected sufficient of the values of 'religious education', or, what is necessary for a child to become a religiously educated person. What needs to be stated clearly are those criteria which must be satisfied before any candidate can be accepted. And for the sake of clarity these criteria may be grouped as (i) dimensional criteria, (ii) educational criteria, and (iii) social criteria.

(i) *Dimensional criteria* By 'dimensional criteria' is meant those criteria stemming from, and reflective of, the meaning of 'religion'. It is tautologous to assert that those activities, procedures and processes deemed to be religiously educational should have to do with the religious dimension of personal life: but in these days when there is so much confusion about what constitutes religious education it is no empty tautology.[5]

Fundamental to any theory of religious education, in terms of determining dimensional criteria for justifying its general aims, is a clear and coherent analysis of the generic concept of 'religion' – and such will be attempted in chapter 3. Suffice it to say at this stage that that analysis will emphasize that 'religion'

18

is unintelligible without some advertence to the spiritual in life and we may thus argue that the general aims of religious education must reflect spiritual values such as are manifested in the multiplicity and variety of religious faiths.

It is not simply insufficient but basically incorrect for general aims in religious education to state that any approach to the task is acceptable if children are encouraged simply to become active moral agents, good citizens or tolerant humanists. Ultimately the general aims of religious education must give practicable direction to the provocation of spiritual insights – and the argument to support this assertion is to be stated in the rest of this book.

(ii) *Educational criteria*   Of the 'educational criteria' which general aims must satisfy the one dominant criterion is the advocacy of depth and breadth of religious understanding, and of scholarly understanding of religious phenomena, contributing to an understanding of man's position and status in this world. Such a criterion necessarily implies the acquisition of relevant knowledge, attitudes and sensitivities because without these the deepening of understanding is impossible.

The one thing the general aims of religious education need not satisfy is any demand for religious faith on the part of the pupils. It need not preclude it either. The fact is that religious education is possible in either case. These ideas, like those concerning 'dimensional criteria' will be worked out in succeeding chapters.

(iii) *Social criteria*   There are two other criteria which all general aims must satisfy in any area of education in a democratic system of state education. First, such aims must be acceptable to a majority of those elected representatives of informed opinion who are responsible for the provision and management of education in county schools. (I am assuming here that county schools are in fact places of education. If this is shown to be otherwise then obviously such a criterion of state *education* is irrelevant – but not of *schooling*.) Second, such aims must be morally acceptable. It is in terms of this criterion that many opponents of religious education in county schools voice their most strident protests when they perceive such 'education' being used for purposes of 'conversion' or 'indoctrination' – and in this way they are right to make their protests. Children, captive in school, are potential persons: and a person is an autonomous being. To treat a child as if he were necessarily and inevitably going to be a member of one's own *congregatio fidelium* is surreptitiously to deny the possibility of his deciding otherwise. And to attempt to take away such a possibility by dint of influence and superior knowledge is to deny his potential autonomy. Such behaviour is immoral.

The employment of these criteria enables one to select the desirable from the unworthy among the numerous general aims suggested for religious education. But even when it has been decided what ought to be the general aims for religious education there still remains the task of justifying the other three kinds of aim. Table 1.2 attempts to summarize the geography of such justifications and thereby, it is hoped, makes them more intelligible.

Table 1.2 *Logical geography of justification of aims in religious education*

Kind of aim	Justified in terms of
General	(i) the standards and values implicit in the meaning of 'religious education' (ii) public acceptability (iii) moral principles
Stage	(i) the general aims (ii) practical recommendations inferred from findings in child psychology
Scheme	(i) the general and stage aims (ii) age, ability and aptitudes of pupils (iii) knowledge and skills of teacher (iv) school environment
Lesson	(i) the general, stage and scheme aims – particularly the last (ii) time limits imposed by physical organization and by children's ability

We began this chapter by stressing the practical necessity of having aims and being clear about them. From this we turned to a consideration of what ought to be the aims in religious education and argued that such a question can only be answered in the light of some understanding of the different kinds of aim necessary to religious education. Whatever the answer given, however, it must always include some reference to general aims and these in turn must satisfy particular criteria.

Such criteria are derived from our understanding of key notions such as 'education' and 'religion' and to the ways in which activities which constitute religious education differ from those classified as 'religious conversion' and 'religious edification'. In becoming clear about what ought to be the aims in religious education we must beware any 'ecclesiastical hangover' which bewitches us into thinking that the religiously educated person is necessarily also a religious believer, and that the task of the religious educator is identical with that of either the priest or the evangelist. On the other hand we must be clear about what is required of the religious educator if his work is to be genuinely religious. To this end we may begin to tussle with the notions of 'education' and 'religion' in the next two chapters.

Chapter 2

Education, conversion and edification

Education, instead of imposing upon us the verdicts of others, commits us more entirely to the task of producing the knowledge of right and wrong from our own personal insight.

J. Oman: *Grace and Personality*

Introduction

It may be fairly argued that the history of religious education in the state system of education from the middle of the nineteenth century until today is that of a long drawn-out battle in which both religious and secular bodies have skirmished to gain control and thus to decide both the content and status of the subject in the curriculum of the county school. What is worse, the weapons employed have often been those of well-entrenched doctrinal and ideological standpoints rather than any appertaining to the necessary requirements of religious education in county schools. The result has been that a good many people have regarded the teaching of religion in schools with suspicion, often seriously questioning its educative value, and parliament has had to single it out from all other subjects and ring it round with statutory provision in Education Acts.

Writing of the reorganization of the national system of education at the beginning of this century, for example, Cruickshank comments that 'the religious question was the most intricate and thorny problem to be faced'[1] and this 'religious question' had to do both with the control of schools and the kind of religious education given in them. As regards the latter.[2]

There were two distinct theories of the function of religion in the schools: 'the religious atmosphere theory' and 'the regulated hours theory'. The first was held by members of the Roman Catholic minority. It was held by many Anglicans who wanted the Church 'atmosphere' to permeate the entire life of the school, who desired, in the words of Lord Hugh Cecil, 'schools with two doors', one leading to the world and the other leading to membership of the worshipping community. On the other hand, some Anglicans held that dogmatic instruction and secular teaching were completely separate. Indeed, in the past Churchmen of this school of thought had pointed to the Conscience Clause as a complete protection for Nonconformist children attending their schools, and had even solicited Nonconformist support for them on the purely secular ground of economy.

This 'religious question' was thus as much a matter of skirmishing between the denominations of the Christian Church as between ecclesiastical and secular bodies and undoubtedly this has faded during the present century as the ecumenical movement has gained ground. But the argument about whether religious education should be Christian education or not, or whether the task of the teacher of religion is that of spiritual director and representative of a particular *congregatio fidelium* or not, persists. In the Sheffield Report of 1961[3] the question was raised, 'What exactly do we want young people to get out of religious education [p. 6]?' and in tackling the question stress was laid 'on the value of Church membership, which was fundamental to the success of the teaching of religious education in the school [p. 7].' Furthermore,

It was agreed that the Christian teacher's aim was that of his Church: that all men should hear the Gospel, learn to love God in Christ, to serve Him and enjoy Him for ever.

23

The teacher's weekly contacts with the children in his charge should be stepping stones on the way to this total committal of each boy or girl to God [p. 14].

Here is a very clear assertion of the 'religious atmosphere' theory all over again and should it be believed that this was representative of only a small minority of people concerned with religious education then it is not without significance to study as 'official' a document as the Plowden Report of 1966.[4] The Report stated the belief held by the majority of the members of the Central Advisory Council for Education 'that religious education and the Act of Worship should influence the entire curriculum and set the tone of living and learning for the whole school community [vol. 1, p. 203]'.

This, of course, says nothing about any particular religion being the one influence upon the curriculum and tone of the school but in discussing the difficulties of the present position of religious education in the primary school the authors distinguish only between Christians and non-Christians either as parents or teachers [p. 205]. This seems to indicate clearly which religion is being borne in mind as influencing the school and such an inference is strengthened when one reads that 'They (young children) should be taught to know and love God' and 'They should not be confused by being taught to doubt before faith is established [p. 207].' If this is not another clear assertion of the 'religious atmosphere' theory of religious education in county schools it is at least a sonorous echo of it.

In much of the thinking about religious education in county schools two assumptions are often implicit if not explicit. The first is that religious education is concerned with children becoming members of some *congregatio fidelium* – hence the task is interpreted and understood as one of religious conversion, religious induction, nurture and edification. The second is that religious education is in fact Christian education – and 'Christian' in particular sectarian terms, whether these be Roman Catholic, Anglican or Nonconformist. Any philosophy of religious education must therefore clearly establish the necessary logical distinctions which subsist between those activities which are educational, conversional and edificatory. And in so far as it is the religious education of persons which concerns us so the establishment of these distinctions may well be rooted in some remarks about 'persons'.

1   The concept of Person

(i) *Persons, human beings and individuals*   Any analysis of the concept of 'person' is fraught with difficulties but a start might be made by noting the necessary distinctions between 'persons', 'human beings' and 'individuals'. It is a tautology that one particular person is an individual person; but the quality of individuality is not necessarily personal. That which is individual is that which is identifiably particular within a group, species or category. Thus a stone, a particular rabbit or the Parthenon are all individuals (and the Christian God and Moslem Allah are not) in so far as they are members of a class of similar referents. Thus the concept 'person' need not imply 'individual person': indeed, the question of the identity of any particular person is other than the analysis of the concept 'person'.

We must return to the matter of the identification of individual persons later and in the meantime note that a distinction is regularly drawn between human beings as a species, and persons as a class, in everyday affairs at home, in business, in hospitals and in the law courts. Whilst all human beings are either regarded as persons or as potential persons, it is nevertheless true that some human beings who fall into the latter class are considered to be actually less than persons. Thus the baby in the cot, the lunatic in the asylum, the senile in the geriatric ward and the psychopath in the law court are held not to be responsible for their actions in the same way as persons. Neither moral nor legal judgments are relevant to them and their abnormal behaviour is excused. Their humanity cannot be denied: but they are recognized as not being persons.

(ii) *The person as an individual mind*   This commonplace distinction between the species 'human being' and the class of 'person' has led many to opine that it is the very feature which human beings possess only potentially, and which persons possess actually, that is implicitly referred to in the concept

25

'person'. This feature is 'mind': that is, a mind sufficiently well-developed that thought may be rational in the sense of controlling one's own self-determination in accordance with acknowledged values. Such a mind is not necessarily either an educated or a learned mind. Instead it is a coherent and realistic self-consciousness.

That the concept of 'person' is satisfactorily explicated in terms of 'mind' is perhaps most clearly stated in Western philosophy in the Cartesian notion of the self as *res cogitans*.[5] For Descartes a person is in essence 'a thinking thing' whose body is an accident. As an observable phenomenon man is an embodied soul: and in 'personal' terms it is not the case that each physical man is a person who has a mind but rather that each person is a mind which happens to have a body.

The idea that a person is a self-conscious soul whose fulfilment is necessarily brought about by cognitive reflection and contemplation is thoroughly Platonic if not older and, despite the growth of empiricistic attitudes and presuppositions, it survives today. Both the atheistic existentialist and the theistic Thomist maintain that, whilst the 'animal' nature of man may not be denied, nevertheless his authentic nature as a person is a product of form-giving thought. And even if a massive difference between these two proponents is that the existentialist teaches that true personality is that which each forges through his own decision-taking, whilst the theist stresses that the nature of a person is as it is in accordance with the form-giving thought of God, nevertheless both identify the enduring worth of man as a person in other than physical terms and as an individual soul at that.

Any analysis of the concept of 'person' solely in terms of 'individual mind' both raises logical problems of a high order and flies in the face of experience, however. The logical problems stem from the inevitably isolated and solipsistic position of the person and are evident in the traditional philosophical 'problem of other minds'. In addition there arise problems of psycho-physical causality 'within' man as well as 'between' men because it is common experience – as well as scientific theory – that mind and body do interact in a variety of ways both in health and disease. Furthermore, the ethical dictates consequent upon such an analysis have an element of the bizarre about them since both a libertine approach of physical self-indulgence to life, and an intensely ascetic programme of physical self-denial, are logically in accord with the acceptance of the analysis of the concept of 'person' as 'individual mind'.

(iii) *The person as an individual body*   Each of these difficulties by itself may not be damning but taken in concert they do suggest that the analysis is inadequate. That some reference to 'mind' in the analysis of 'person' is required seems to be utterly necessary but to identify persons simply in terms of mind – and 'individual mind' at that – is to be rejected as insufficient. Indeed, under the diverse influence of both Judaeo-Christian thought, with its emphasis upon man as an ensouled body, and of modern scientific thought, with its justifiable obsession with empirical data, it is nowadays often accepted that as much emphasis must be placed upon the individual body in any analysis of the concept 'person'.

This awareness of the importance of the physical dimension in personal life has been instrumental in suggesting an analysis of the concept of person in purely bodily terms. Such a concept of person as 'body', together with its emphasis upon assessment of personal behaviour in terms of overt physical phenomena, is implicit in the work of behaviourist psychologists, in the thinking of politicians and ideologists who preach a policy of human satisfaction in possession of material things, and in the theories of those philosophers who reduce mental phenomena to the status of qualitative assessments of public physical performances.[6]

That the spatio-temporal limitations of the body are the physical individuations of each distinct human being cannot be denied: but any understanding of a human being as a person can never be summed-up in physical terms alone. No one can deny the importance of the physical dimension of personal life without unworldly sophistry: but to attempt a reduction of talk about 'persons' to purely physicalistic terms is to deny the validity of human experience and to be logically naïve or deceitful. Consistently conspicuous in all accounts of human beings who are persons is the insight that 'man cannot live by bread alone': and the philosophical inquiries of two thousand years and more are unanimous in declaring that pertinent application of terms to persons requires more, and other than, purely physical referents.

(iv) *The person as a social being* Neither an understanding of persons solely in 'mental' terms, nor an analysis of the concept simply in 'bodily' conditions is acceptable. And if either is propounded in such a way as to suggest that 'person' necessarily implies a wholly separate, individual mind or body, then such must be emphatically rejected because what must never be lost sight of is the necessary social dimension of being a person. In the realm of mental phenomena overwhelming evidence forces the conclusion that a person's mind is as much a social phenomenon as an individual innate structure: and the growing understanding of symbiotic relationships drives one to conclude that a body is as dependent upon other bodies for its continued existence as for its origin.

Part of what is meant by 'person' is advertence to relations which subsist between a human being on the one hand and his social milieu on the other hand. To be a person is at least to be a social being. In Temple's words,[7]

> I am in essence a member of society. Membership of family and nation is not an accidental appendage of my individuality, but a constitutive element of it. . . . Membership is a fact of our nature, and the essence of obligation is its expression.

Strictly speaking, the atheist alone on the desert island is not fully a person: and there was more sanity and less eccentricity than might be imagined in the behaviour of the colonial official who, alone 'up country' except for the company of his native servants, dressed for dinner.

The importance of the social dimension in personal life is so great that there is no small temptation to believe that 'person' *means* 'social being'. But a distinction often insisted upon – and rarely clarified – in ethical theories is one which needs to be borne in mind in any analysis of the concept person – *viz*. that between a 'person' and a 'role-player'. It is to be regretted that this distinction is not always abided by and much sense which is spoken about role-players is transferred indiscriminately to persons.

There can be little doubt that the structures of the particular society in which each human being lives largely determine the ways in which each member of that society relates to other members. The roles we play are not of our individual making but are made available to us within the social milieu. Moreover, the ways in which a role may be played are largely limited by social forces. This, of course, is hardly a novel, or even a modern insight. As long ago as the first century AD Epictetus noted in *Encheiridion*:[8]

> Remember that you are an actor in a play, the character of which is determined by the playwright: if He wishes the play to be short, it is short, if long, it is long; if He wishes you to play the part of a beggar, remember to act even this role adroitly; and so if your role be that of a cripple, an official, or a layman. For this is your business, to play admirably the role assigned you: but the selection of that role is Another's.

When the sociologist considers man's standing as a social being, and only as a social being, then necessarily he can only describe him in terms of role-playing. Such is a legitimate sociological advertence to man. Unfortunately this legitimate description of the social facet of man is sometimes taken as an adequate account of man as a person. And when sociological thinking is accompanied by political commitment to some form of all-embracing socialism then the understanding of the human person in terms of a socially-determined structural essence is given the authoritative stamp of an ideological *imprimatur*.

To be a person is to be a social being and not an isolated windowless monad. But it is not to be simply and solely a social being who is a role-player. The meaning of 'person' is to be elucidated in terms other than those of social parameters alone because the degree to which, and the manner in which, each makes something of these social parameters for himself is other than the social determinants themselves. It is persons who play roles, and not that persons are role-players. One and the same person may take on and put off new and old roles without necessarily changing as a person. Indeed a change of role (e.g. in employment) is other than, and different from, a personal revolution (e.g. a religious conversion): and one of these changes does not always and necessarily imply the other.

(v) *The person as an autonomous being* The argument as it stands is that 'person' implies both mental and physical conditions, and each of these conditions, both separately and in concert, are in some major degree social in nature. At the minimum, therefore, the concept of 'person' implies some complex social status such that social relations are necessary to personal existence. This being so, it follows that 'person' may imply either that the grid, or pattern, of such relations is heteronomously inflicted upon whatever is personal, or that the formation and constitution of such relations is a matter of autonomous decision. It is the former which is implicit in those analyses of 'person' which emphasize the role-playing character of persons: and it is the latter which is implicit in analyses which emphasize the thought-giving form of persons – e.g. those of existentialists.

The persuasive strength of the latter lies in the fact that persons are held to be responsible for their actions unless exceptional conditions pertain. Such is both illogical and unfair unless what is meant by 'person' is that which is self-conscious, self-directing and self-organizing. One may be held to be a responsible agent if one is an autonomous self and not an heteronomous object: responsible agency can only be ascribed to a subject who hammers out his agency both within and upon social determinants in a reflective, intelligent and purposive manner. And to the extent that such self-government is denied, either by dint of psychosomatic circumstances or political organization, so it is generally believed that one is debased as a person. That which is essential for a human being to be a person is the freedom and ability to determine his own limits: and thus it is no contradiction to assert that a person may behave both as a brute beast and as an angel.

Such responsible self-government is psycho-physical in nature. But it has already been argued that both mind and body are as much socially determined as self-directed. It follows necessarily, therefore, that implicit in the notion of 'person' is not simply private autonomy but public determination.

30

At the very least, that which is personal is private-public, subjective-objective. And this must not be taken to mean separate private features alongside differing public contributions within a compendium or conglomerate, but rather an interdepending and unified fusing such that neither the privacy nor publicity of the whole is entirely separable. This is no denial of the fact that in academic studies – say, biological, psychological or sociological – private and public features may be separated out for purposes of convenient study. Instead, what is being asserted is that if, and when, man is regarded in 'personal' terms then he must necessarily be regarded as private-public, autonomous-heteronomous subject-object.

(vi) *The person as a multi-dimensional harmony* Academic studies of man-in-society are necessarily fragmentary in view of their differing logics but implicit in the notion of 'person' as private-public is the sense of unity. The beauty of academic study is that it enriches our understanding of the diverse richness and rich diversity of personal nature. The picture which emerges is not an abstract monotone slab but a colourful, multi-faceted, multi-dimensional form. The personal in life is diverse and complex: it is cognitive and emotional, spiritual and physical, moral and prudential, historical and contemporary, local and universal. And these diverse dimensions harmonize and unify in the person.

To be a person is to be a diversified unit and a unified diversity. Diversity without integration is fragmentation: and singleness without complexity is vacuity and emptiness. That which is personal is not fragmentary and vacuous but is instead that which is harmonious and significant. And such harmony is true subjectivity, authentic autonomy, because it is of the creative spirit of man ever determining his own being in active communion and union with the diverse multiplicity of academically isolable entities which confront him both 'beyond' and 'within'. Hence man's longing for active peace which is 'completeness' and an absence of fragmenting confrontation – in Jewish terms, shalom.

The supposition that an account of man acceptable in one academic discipline is an adequate account of man as a person is incorrect. It is only partially true that a person is a rational

31

being, or a social unit, or a being with supracosmic destiny, or simply a highly evolved animal, or a unique being with conceptual thought which can now determine its own evolution. As a person man is all these things in unified harmony: and his individual identity as a person is a matter of the complex harmony of these many facets and dimensions. A thumb-print may individuate a particular human body but it does not identify a particular person. As mentioned earlier, the law courts are careful to distinguish between persons who must be held responsible for their actions and unfortunate human beings who are not fully personal. And whilst the thumb-print may identify the body of the man, if he did not know what he was doing in 'committing a crime', or genuinely did not recognize the difference between what is right and what is wrong, then the court would not treat him as a person, but only as a potential person.

That which is recognizable as an individual person is a complex harmony of beliefs, actions, relations, dispositions, habits and skills as well as physical features because a person is a multi-dimensional unit and not simply a monolithic physical particular.

(vii) *Person and selfhood* Such an understanding of the notion of 'person' necessarily reduces to the status of pseudo-question all those hoary problems which have been raised concerning the nature of the 'self'. The logic of the notion 'self' is necessarily that of a polar relation to that of the notion 'other', and the problems which have arisen in identifying the 'self' have usually been consequent upon implicit assumptions about 'person' such that only one of the dimensions of personhood is regarded as truly personal. Moreover any particular understanding of the one dimension selected has confounded the confusion: and as the understanding of anything is rooted in metaphysical beliefs so the identification of the self has more often reflected the metaphysical outlook of the enquirer than the actual nature of persons. Thus Aristotle's identification of the 'self' as 'rational mind' is consequent upon the metaphysical presupposition that the entire universe, and all things in it, is an epiphenomenal manifestation of rational principles, the Logos. And Marx's concept of the 'self' as a social unit is likewise consequent upon some vague presuppositions about the 'material' and upon the belief in the generation of consciousness through social interplay.

Our own understanding of 'person' as a multi-dimensional harmony necessarily determines that the self – as self-conscious – can be, and is, nothing more and nothing less than this same one. I as a person am the self that I am: my person and my self are one and the same. The identifiable individuality of personhood which is ascribed to me is my self. And this is logically necessary because what distinguishes a man who is a person from a human being who is not a person (or even an animal) is an intense self-consciousness. 'Person' implies an integrated unity of diverse dimensions, facets and functions in the highest form of consciousness – that is, consciousness not simply of 'external' others but consciousness of the self as being conscious of itself as itself. Personhood involves such self-consciousness: but personhood also refers to complex harmony. Personal self-consciousness is therefore consciousness of the self as an integrated diverse whole – not of some single strand within the twisted rope of personhood.

(viii) *Metaphysical presuppositions*   The metaphysical presupposition that 'mind' and 'matter' are so utterly different and distinct that they cannot properly cause effects in each other underlies a good many attempts to identify the 'self' with but one dimension of personhood. If the essence of 'mind' is 'conscious freedom', and that of 'matter' is 'unconscious mechanical determinism' then obviously the assertion that they cannot cause effects in each other is necessary. But in the last one hundred years psycho-analysts have suggested that the mind is far more 'determined' than previously imagined: and scientists have shied away from a mechanistic paradigm of the starry heavens above and have begun to embrace notions of 'matter' of a relational randomness and statistical correlation of impulses which deny the repetitive 'static stuffiness' of the universe. So both absolute freedom of the mind and total determinacy of matter seem no longer tenable as metaphysical principles with which to conduct any debate about persons.

Those metaphysical principles and cosmological beliefs which are implicit in our notion of a person as 'subject-object' are those which stem from Whitehead's Philosophy of Organism.[9] The fundamental metaphysical category is that of 'creativity' – that is, the notion of pure activity underlying the nature of things and thinghood which is at one and the same time the urge both towards differentiation and unification, variety and harmony. As pure activity it is uncharacterized and beyond categorization being the ultimate generality which is present in all classes and objects. And seeing that everything which exists is grounded in 'pure activity' so the whole universe is in a state of 'becoming' such that Nature is not to be regarded as a chance conglomeration of permanent 'bits of matter' but as an interrelated network of events which are constantly coming into being and perishing. The universe is conceived as an 'organism' rather than a 'machine' and it has no static structure but is constantly 'in process'.

That which determines the continuing, unifying process of the universe is the interaction of its many parts in accordance with the creative principle whereby each successive phase is not so much an imitative repetition of what has gone before (a fact of which historians have long been aware) but a newly created replication of the past. The future is not divorced from the past, nor the past from the future: but here in the present the future is forged out of the past, not by dint of 'abstraction' or simple 'derivation' but through creation of a new one, distinct yet related.

All phenomena are to be understood in terms of 'creative interaction'. Each entity both contributes to the process of another's becoming and is itself constructed and constituted according to the way it feels its objective world. As a prehending thing a phenomenon is intelligible only as part of an extensive network of interwoven events: and the uniqueness of each created synthesis lies in the manner of its powers of prehension. So the 'picture' of the universe which is jettisoned is that of a mechanical continuation of repetitive patterns of indestructible particles. Instead there is substituted a conception of the cosmos in which each of its various parts act upon each other, and react to each other, each according to its powers and potential in a creative – i.e. an 'active becoming' – manner. Each member of the universe is a 'continuing interactor'.

(ix) *The person as an objective self-integrator*   In these terms our notion of a person is that of a complex, multidimensional interactor, a creature whose unifying synthesis lies, like all interactors, in the manner of its powers of prehension. Such powers, in the case of persons, are those of apprehension both of others and of the self as creative interactors. Thus the person knows himself as a person to be both an autonomous and an heteronomous being. 'The deep significance of the self is its interaction with a world on which it depends, yet, of which nevertheless it should be independent.'[10]

Being self-conscious, a person not only knows what is the case but also entertains notions of what might be. He is a creatively conscious agent who, to a large extent, can determine his own interaction but any interaction he undertakes, or permits, will only be felicitous in so far as it abides by his own becoming nature together with the nature of that with which he interacts, or intends to interact. It follows, therefore, that the values implicit in the choices a person makes have an ontological core of deep significance such that ultimately they must be objective.

A person's goodness and well-being is therefore both a private and public matter: his subjectivity and objectivity are of a kind.[11]

> Only by being true to ourselves can we find the reality we must absolutely follow; yet, only by the sense of reality we must absolutely follow can we be true to ourselves. Thus our dependence and our independence would seem to be apart merely as strands of one cord which have no strength except united.

The meaning of 'person' is, then, that such is a value-centred harmony of self-conscious interaction whose values are not entirely of his own choosing. True personal autonomy is not simply choice of path of action but self-determination by dint of self-surrender to the necessary reality of creative becoming by way of interaction. And the identity of the person is not established simply by reference solely to a particular body, a particular set of beliefs or particular courses of action, but to the whole ongoing pattern of self-directed reality-controlled interaction on many fronts in unified harmony.

35

To be a self-conscious, self-directing and self-organizing being is necessarily to be one who is conscious of the future in terms of having intentions which can only be 'worked out' in the future and in terms of understanding what needs to be done in the present in order that whatever is possible in the future may be achieved. Thus a person is an intentional agent – and this notion necessarily implies the temporal connotations of both present and future. A person's intentional agency is necessarily of the present but its pertinence and significance is void unless it is also understood in terms of the future.

As a self-integrating interactor a person is in a state of creative becoming, not one of fossilized staticity, and therefore the maintenance of his present subsistence as an identifiable person – as a *self-integrating* interactor – necessarily requires a consciousness of agency which has both present reality and future possibilities. The whole notion of 'creative becoming' as applied to a self-conscious creature necessarily implies having and implementing intentions. Thus Ishiguro is correct in asserting that[12]

> a being who fails to think of any state of affairs in the future which he sets out to bring about, and has no awareness at any time of what he is doing which carries some reference to the future, cannot properly be described as a person.

Personal identity is therefore a matter of recognition of an ongoing pattern of self-directed reality-controlled interaction on many fronts in terms of unified intentional agency. A particular person is a particular self-conscious interacting agent, a particular objective self-integrator.

2 Induction and conversion

In so far as subjects are intentional agents, and inasmuch as such agency is necessarily objective self-integration, so those activities which are concerned with the conversion, edification and education of persons are necessarily concerned in some way or another with objective self-integration. The logical differences between these forms of activity lie in the precise nature of their contribution to objective self-integration, or, to subjective agency.

(i) *The establishment of faith* It has already been noted in the Introduction to this chapter that the authors of the Plowden Report were aware of the possibility of establishing religious faith in young children. Such a process, whereby children are nurtured and brought up in a particular religious way of life, may be termed 'induction'. When adolescent children and young people are brought to a particular way of living religiously such a reorientation may be termed 'conversion'.[13] In either inductional or conversional activities the intention is the same – *viz*. the establishment of religious faith.

Now 'faith' is not a particular feature of any one dimension of personhood: it is, for example, neither intellectual credence nor simply emotional reaction. Faith is that matrix of disposition, attitude and action in which a person expresses his entire self as a subject. Faith is the exercise of subjective agency: it is the committal of one's entire self as a whole person. Thus 'faith' is commonly expressed in terms of 'trust' because 'trust' is the disposing of oneself, even to the point of endangering oneself.

In terms of objective self-integration, faith is a matter of active and conscious committal to a particular pattern of reality-controlled interaction. Because a personal subject only exists as an active agent so active commitment of oneself is a necessary requirement of being a person. But of significance in such subjective committal is the degree of certainty which is always present in all commitment. No action or endeavour can ever be undertaken with that degree of confidence which may be termed 'total certainty': yet to live as a person – as an intentional agent – requires active agency on one's part. Thus to live as a person is always to act in the absence of total justification and often in spite of contrary evidence. As Newman put it: 'Life is for action. If we insist on proofs for everything, we shall never come to action: to act you must assume, and that assumption is faith.'[14]

To be a person is to be objectively self-integrating: to be objectively self-integrating is to commit oneself to a particular pattern of reality-controlled interaction: but to commit oneself to any particular pattern of subjective agency is a matter of faith. Thus it has often been opined that a person cannot live without a faith: and those who are responsible for the welfare of children and young people have rightly intuited that the future generation in their charge should have 'a faith by which to live'.

(ii) *A pattern of integration* This correct intuition of a logical necessity of personal life assists in making intelligible the oft-repeated reduction of religious education to religious induction and/or religious conversion. The intention is admirable and worthy. It is an attempt to enable children grown to adults to live fully personal lives (and not simply human lives) – to be 'masters of their own ship' and not to be 'corks tossed about by the waves'.

The danger implicit in religious inductional and conversional activities, however, is that of imposing a particular pattern of integration which, whilst it may be objective, may not be self-directed. Authentic personal interaction is self-integration: genuine conversion is self-surrender. And, as will be argued later, religious education is concerned with enabling children so to surrender themselves to any particular pattern of religious faith if they so wish, rather than directing them to one pattern of objective self-integration.

The contribution which inductional and conversional activities make to subjective agency is to provide a particular way or path of objective self-integration which lays down a 'blue-print' whereby the many dimensions of personhood may be united in a whole and healthy harmony of personhood. In a limited and 'primitive' social milieu where one such pattern for personal life is dominant then such activities might also pass as 'educational'. Where the social milieu is diverse, complex and universal, however, embracing disparate 'ways of life', a clear distinction must be held between such activities on the one hand and educational activities on the other hand.[15] To be converted to Christianity, for example, is to surrender oneself to Christ as one's pattern of objective self-integration: it is to say with Paul, 'I have been crucified with Christ; yet I live; and yet no longer I, but Christ liveth in me.'[16] But to be an educated Christian is all of this and something more.

3 Edification

To surrender oneself to a particular pattern of reality-controlled interaction is but a first step, in much the same way as to walk down the aisle with one's spouse on one's arm is but the beginning of married life. As with all forms of interaction, development and growth are as much features of religious objective self-integration as of any form of faithful commitment. There is a long way to go before the convert becomes a saint, or the student a master, and the religious life is a long time aflowering before the directed becomes a director.

Those activities which are edificatory are those which strengthen and deepen a particular pattern of objective self-integration. This being so, it follows that such harmony is only possible if the objectivity of that with which the self is interacting is known and respected. Any reality-controlled self-determination is only efficacious, ongoing and 'becoming' as long as that with which one is united is treated according to its objective nature. And this is as much true in those activities which purport to be religiously edificatory as in any other kind of edificatory activity.

To take any form of the Christian religion by way of example, edificatory activities are those which assist the strengthening of that form of personal harmony known as 'holiness'. The intention of such activities is to bring about knowledge of God on the part of the individual person so that the initial self-surrender of conversion, whereby personal autonomy is transformed into personal theonomy, is enriched and developed. But such is only possible, of course, if God is respected as God and approached as such by the person who is to be edified.

It is at this point that one begins to observe major differences between conversional and edificatory activities. It is not simply the intentions which are different but the agents and principles also. The intention of conversional activities is that of establishing a pattern of objective self-integration: the agent is one who already pursues such a pattern: and the principle is one of faithful commitment. But if the intention of edificatory activities is that of the growth of holiness by way of unity of the self with God, by way of knowledge of God, then it is God himself who is the agent of edification. God alone can make himself known to man. And he can only do this if man 'puts himself in the way of God'. Thus the principle of the edificatory activity, in Christian terms, is 'love', not faith. As the anonymous author of *The Cloud of Unknowing* put it centuries ago, 'by love can he be caught and held, but by thinking never.'[17]

In many religions edificatory interactions feature mystical paths and practices. But some of us are not of the mystical or contemplative mould and in some organized religious faiths – e.g. Theravada Buddhism – there is a recognized distinction between the contemplative monks and the laity going about their daily lives. For the latter, religious edification is a matter of 'acts of merit', though it is tacitly understood that such are not sufficient for the full flowering of the spiritual life. That is possible for the monk alone.

In other religions, especially those of the Hebraic tradition, moral acts and social works of charity are regarded as forms of interaction crucially constitutive of the growing personal harmony of holiness. 'Pure religion and undefiled before our God and Father is this,' writes James, 'to visit the fatherless and widows in their affliction, and to keep himself unspotted from the world.'[18] Thus for the Jew, Christian and Moslem, objective self-integration is built up through caring and loving works directed towards the whole created order as well as through contemplation and prayer. One is reminded of this in the delightful epitaph of a watchmaker at St Petroch's Church, Lydford in Devon:[19]

Here lies in horizontal position the outside case of George Routleigh, watchmaker, whose abilities in that line were an honour to his profession; integrity was the mainspring and prudence the regulator of all the actions of his life: humane, generous, and liberal, his hand never stopped till he had relieved distress; so nicely regulated were all his movements that he never went wrong except when set a'going by people who did not know his key; even then he was easily set right again. He departed this life, November 14th 1802, aged 57; wound up in hopes of being taken in hand by his Maker, and being thoroughly cleaned, repaired, and set a'going in the world to come.

In many religions mystical practices and social works go hand in hand in building up particular patterns of reality-controlled self-determination: and if religious education is ever to be understood in terms of religious edification then the activities which are organized under the aegis of RE in the schools will have to be accordingly relevant and pertinent.

4 Education

That educational and edificatory activities can be confused is well-known to every experienced RE teacher. This is not surprising because, as Andersen has argued, 'education' and 'edification' are structurally similar ideas in so far as both are instances of the more general category of 'nurture'.[20] But they are not identical notions: and the activities whose aims and intentions accord with the values implicit in each do vary. Accordingly an attempt will now be made to characterize the features of educational activities.

(i) *The person as the educational agent*   It may seem an otiose statement but it is worth remembering that it is persons who educate persons. Non-persons never educate non-persons. Inanimate objects, plants, animals and divine beings are never thought of as educating persons or each other. Neither are they thought of as being either educated or uneducated. Even when God is thought of as 'Person' he is not spoken of as educating, or not educating, his people. As has already been argued, in Christian terms God is the agent in edificatory activities – but it is Christian persons who educate other persons.

There is thus something unique about persons whereby they can educate each other – and only each other. Perhaps the full significance of this point can be expressed by saying that educational activities have to do with that which is uniquely personal – with the feature of persons which marks them off from whatever is non-personal. This feature, it has been argued in section 1, is that, whilst a person is an interactor like all other phenomena in this universe, he is nevertheless an objective self-integrating interactor. He is capable of directing

41

himself but only by integrating his numerous and varied dimensions in accord with objective requirements and criteria.

Educational activities have to do with objective self-integration. This being so, it might be argued that such activities actually promote objective self-integration. But the difficulty with this argument is that if a person is an objective self-integrator, and if educational activities are those which actually promote objective self-integration, then it follows necessarily that one only becomes a person by dint of being educated: and the idea of 'an uneducated person' is a contradiction.[21] This, however, is manifestly absurd.

The difference between educated and uneducated persons is certainly not that one is a person and the other is not. It cannot be that educational activities are the sole means whereby one becomes a person, or even the means whereby one maintains one's personhood. Instead, educational activities are related to objective self-integration in a contributory rather than a causal manner.

(ii) *The intellectual content of educational activities* Educational activities are not unique in contributing to objective self-integration. The mother's nursing of the baby, the girl's teasing of her brother, and the actor's entertainment of his audience may all contribute in their different ways to objective self-integration. What is unique about an educational activity is the particularity of its contribution to personhood and this lies in the fact that an educational activity always has something to do with a person's mind, and especially with a person's intellect. That which is educational is primarily that which is contributory to the advancement of the intellect in the part it may play in objective self-integration. Any activity intended to provoke no intellectual discernment is not educational.

This is no argument that educational activities are solely and only concerned with intellectual advancement but rather that such activities are primarily concerned with it. Indeed, if our analysis of the concept of 'person' is correct then, in so far as a person is a unified harmony of many facets and dimensions, so the advancement of the intellect *in vacuo* as it were is an impossibility. The advancement of a person's intellect is necessarily related to, say, emotional, moral and physical development.

Of all the intellectual virtues it is 'understanding' which is of supreme value. Intellectual activity is as varied as the multifarious interactions in which any one person engages. The number of disparate facts remembered, for example, the variety of beliefs held and the distinct forms of reasoning engaged in by any one agent are such that, without understanding, it would be impossible ever to act as one and the same person, or even to ascribe reponsibilities to any one agent. The reasons for ascribing 'understanding' such primacy and importance will become clear in chapters 4 and 5: suffice it to say at this point that it will be argued there that 'understanding' is 'unifying insight' and is necessary for intellectual cohesion and unity. And the need for such unity cannot be overstressed when it is remembered that 'personhood' implies harmonious unity.

(iii) *The educated person*   Educational activities are those which provoke depth and breadth of understanding,[22] and especially that kind of understanding which aids objective self-integration. Implicit in that assertion is a distinction between what might be termed 'academic' understanding and 'educational' understanding. The former is 'at home' in institutes of higher education and universities where scholars conduct research and pursue knowledge for its own sake. The information gained and understood may have little bearing, or none whatsoever, upon a person's understanding of himself as a person. But this cannot be the case with the understanding provoked in educational activities because if the latter are to contribute to man's objective self-integration then, however important may be the growth of understanding of objective phenomena in their own right, ultimately such insight must be related to man's own position and status as man. Educational activities are those which provoke intelligent consideration of the reflective question, 'What is man?'

Human beings do not become persons by way of educational activities. Instead, the educated man is one whose understanding of himself-in-the-cosmos is so developed that his intellect plays no small part in his necessary objective self-integration as a person. The educated man is not necessarily more firmly committed to a particular pattern of reality-controlled self-determination than his uneducated brother: neither need he be a more harmonious unit. He is not necessarily morally better, spiritually more perfect or physically stronger than the uneducated person: neither are his social relations necessarily happier. Where he differs is in his realization of a developed state of intellectual understanding whereby he perceives with clarity what is necessary for personal life to go forward.

Whether or not an educated man acts on such intellectual discernment is another matter because the intellect is not always in accord with either the will or desires. For this reason it is no contradiction to speak of a particular educated person being an unhappy person or even a renegade: and there is no logical impediment in speaking of certain happy people, together with some saints, as being uneducated.

Educational activities have to do with the promotion of intellectual understanding which may aid objective self-integration: and in so far as there can be public criteria for testing the possession of such understanding so the educational standing of any person may be assessed and compared with that of others. But a person's subjective agency, his particular pattern of objective self-integration, is something other than that because it is more and other than merely the outworking of clarity of insight. As such it is more dependent upon conversional and edificatory activities.

It will be argued in chapter 6 that those activities which are religiously educational play a crucial role in the provocation of a person's understanding of himself-in-the-cosmos. Suffice it to say at the moment we are now able to distinguish with somewhat greater clarity the educational criteria which general aims in religious education must satisfy. They need never satisfy demands for the establishment of religious faith or for growth in the religious life. The over-all intentions of religiously educational activities must be the provocation of intellectual understanding *vis-à-vis* the religious dimension of life: the agent is the religiously educated person: and the principle of the activities is reflective thought in its widest sense. The implications of this, however, can only be drawn out by a

44

careful study of 'religion' as a dimension of personal life, and of a person's understanding. Similarly, any practical recommendations for religious education can only be inferred on the basis of logical analysis of the key concepts 'religion' and 'understanding'.

Chapter 3
The religious dimension of personal life

People often speak of Communism or Nazism as a 'secular religion'. But not all fanaticism is religious. The passions of the total revolutions and total wars which have devastated our age were not religious but moral. Their morality was inverted and became immanent in brute force because a naturalistic view of man forced them into this manifestation.

M. Polanyi: *Beyond Nihilism*

Introduction

Educational activities contribute to objective self-integration by provoking personal understanding of man's position and status in the cosmos. Religiously educational activities are therefore only efficacious if they are pertinently relevant to the religious dimension of personal life. Accordingly those dimensional criteria which partially determine the justifiability of the general aims of religious education stem from a clear understanding of the religious dimension of personal life: and this, in turn, implies an analysis of the concept of 'religion' as applied to personal life.

Any attempt to analyse the concept of religion is fraught with difficulties, however. Many religious believers employ the term in a thoroughly subjective way: and many opponents of organized religious faiths use it pejoratively. And its metaphorical uses seem legion in number. Furthermore, there is often confusion of the task of the philosopher attempting to analyse the concept with that of other scholars studying the phenomenon of religion according to the dictates of their own particular field. Accordingly it may be profitable to spell out briefly the task which is to be undertaken here.

Let us begin with an analogy. Some horticultural produce is termed 'fruit' and some is termed 'vegetable' and, as well as being enjoyed at the table, such produce may be studied in all manner of ways. The historian may trace the story of the potato from its arrival in Western Europe in the sixteenth century from the Americas: the geneticist may attempt to explain the production of infertile hybrid plants: and the agriculturalist may study ways of increasing production.

On the other hand there may arise questions about whether a particular produce is to be classified as a fruit or a vegetable and in the end no amount of detailed inspection of the actual produce will settle the question simply because it is a question as much about what is meant by 'fruit' and 'vegetable' as about common characteristics which are observable in either the fruit or the vegetable. Faced with the puzzle of whether a particular plant is fruit or vegetable one has to do as much hard thinking about the concepts of 'fruit' and 'vegetable' as one has to indulge in detailed inspection of the plant.

In a similar way 'religion' may be studied from various academic standpoints. The historian may trace the activities of religious believers in past events: the apologist may put forward a reasoned defence of one particular religious faith: the phenomenologist may trace patterns of common characteristics in numerous religions: and the psychologist and sociologist may attempt to provide us with causal explanations of how people become religious. But presupposed in all these studies is the exact identification of the religious as distinct from the non-religious or the irreligious and, like 'fruit' and 'vegetable', such an identification involves as much hard thinking about the concept of religion as it does careful observation of the phenomena of religion. Indeed, unless one is clear about what is meant by 'religion' there is no guarantee that religious phenomena will be recognized as such even when they confront one. And there can be no discussion of the validity of any purported general aims of religious education if there is confusion of thought about the dimensional criteria which have to be satisfied and which are reflective of the exact meaning of 'religion'.

If our efforts to religiously educate children are to be efficacious we must work with a clear and coherent concept of religion as implicit in the phrase 'the religious dimension of life'.[1] Clarity of thought is necessary for practical efficiency: and in our thinking we must advert to the religious dimension of personal life because all educational activities provoke intellectual understanding of personal life. At the very least, the specific task of explicit religious education is therefore the arousal in the children of sensitivity to themselves as potentially religious persons. And for the teacher this implies a clear grasp of the logic of the *religious* dimension of personal life.

1 The religious dimension of personal life

(i) *Its spirituality*   As with all dimensions of personal life so the religious dimension is part of the constant self-conscious interaction which constitutes each individual person. But what makes the religious dimension so particular is that it is through and through spiritual. This is no tacit argument that other dimensions of life have no spiritual element: instead, what is being affirmed is that of all the dimensions of personal life the religious dimension is entirely spiritual. Both that element of man's nature involved in each person's interaction with his environment, and that element in the environment with which each person interacts in the religious dimension of life is spiritual: and it is only valuable in so far as it aids further spiritual interaction. Hence our previous remark (chapter 1, section 2) that in the religious life the path is the prize.

In contrast to such a characterization of the religious dimension of life as through and through spiritual attention may be drawn to all the physical accompaniments of 'world religions', to all the traditional physical practices, rites and rituals, to all the intellectual constructs and rationalizations of religion. And it may be argued that religion is to be characterized by reference to these observable phenomena rather than by reference to something as elusive as the spirit. Such, however, is to be blinded by the trees and to miss the wood.

The fact is that, from the religious standpoint, all these observable phenomena are only of instrumental value as aids and guides to the spiritual life. No one can deny their value as such in organized religious faiths, nor can their presence be regarded necessarily as evidence of 'bad' religion because a person is as much a physical and mental creature as a spiritual being. Indeed, in a phenomenological study of the world's religions equal value would have to be given to both overt behavioural data and inner emotions, dispositions and experiences. As Sangharakshita says of Buddhism, for example, 'The ideal account would in fact show spiritual experiences crystallizing into concrete doctrinal and disciplinary forms and these resolving themselves back into spiritual experiences. Full justice would then be done both to the letter and the spirit of the tradition.'[2] But what makes Buddhism a vehicle for the religious dimension of personal life is not its letter but its spirit.

To understand what is meant by 'religion' in 'religious education' therefore – as opposed to indulging in a phenomenological study of the world's religions – our attention must be focused upon spirituality. And if we can become clear about the concept in these terms then we shall be in a better position to state the dimensional criteria for determining general aims in religious education and also thereby identify the particular contribution which religious education can make to objective self-integration.

(ii) *The meaning of 'spirit'*   The key term is thus the 'spirit': and in characterizing the religious dimension of personal life as spiritual three meanings, three connotations, are constantly present and consistently intertwined.

First, the spiritual is other than the physical. It is neither limited by considerations of space and time nor is it open to demonstration by way of pieces of apparatus. In this sense the spiritual is a common feature of everyday life because, whilst one can make sense of many physical features of life in terms of bio-chemical reactions and cause-and-effect events, the total personal life is not entirely of this order. Loving, feeling, hoping, perceiving, thinking, giving – to name but a few

49

features of personal life – are only intelligible in terms both of the physical and of the spiritual. In this sense of 'spiritual', attention is being drawn to the invisible and the intangible in life – but not to the unreal.

The second connotation of 'spiritual' is that to be intuited by means of contrast with the mental rather than the physical. Here the stress is upon the non-rationality of the spiritual in everyday life. That which is of the spirit in this sense is ultimately that which is beyond strict, succinct terminological expression because it is beyond accurate conceptualization and beyond rational demonstration and logical proof and disproof. So when man does attempt to rationalize about the things of the spirit he employs concepts which are 'logically odd' and he makes use of patterns of speech which are paradoxical, poetic, mythic and parabolic rather than prosaic. It is because spiritual matters are non-rational (not irrational) that human articulation hints at rather than grasps the spiritual, and veils as much as it reveals.[3]

The third connotation of 'spirit' is most positive. It is that to be found in our talk about 'spirited horses', 'petroleum spirit' and those alcoholic beverages known as 'spirits'. It is the sense of restless energy, dynamic activity, hard-bridled power and effervescence. Such is the meaning explicit in the etymology of the word – from the Latin *spiritus*, meaning 'breath' or 'wind': and, at that, the gasp of the athlete as he lunges for the tape rather than the sigh of the lovelorn maid, and the gale-force wind rather than the breeze of a summer's evening. (From the Greek equivalent, *pneuma*, we derive 'pneumonia' and 'pneumatic' with their connotations of 'power'.) Thus the spiritual in life is the dynamic: and a spiritual interaction is liable to be disturbingly energetic.

(iii) *The mysteries of the spirit*   The religious dimension of life is therefore complex in so far as it is always non-physical, non-rational and dynamic. As such it is necessarily rooted in and directly concerned with the mysterious in life: that is, not the mysterious which is a problem which may one day be solved by, say, the detective, the mathematician or the geneticist, but rather the mysterious which is the ultimate depths of personal life.

There is undoubtedly some debate among scholars as to whether we 'intuit' these mysteries, 'contuit' them alongside contingent physical phenomena,[4] or are alerted to them by 'signals of transcendence'[5] but what is not to be doubted is that the religious dimension of life is that dimension which is bound up with these spiritual mysteries. In the main there are four areas of such mystery, each separate but not unrelated. First, there is the mystery of the fundamental nature of being – why there is anything at all in existence. Second, there is the apparent antinomy, or contradiction, of spontaneity and co-ordination in the universe – why so much apparently freely chosen interaction does not result in chaos and destruction. Third, there is the mystery of teleology and dysteleology – why so much purposive action often seems so purposeless in the long run. And, finally, there is the mystery of the ultimate grounding of value – why the universe has the particular values it has rather than others.[6]

The religious dimension of life is singularly associated with these spiritual mysteries of life: and organized religious faiths attempt to offer patterns of objective self-integration in the face of them. Thus the complexity of the religious dimension of life is partially that of its 'mysteriousness': and such complexity is recognized as intense when once it is realized that such spiritual mysteries confront man both 'beyond' and 'within'.

(iv) *The 'meaning-giving' function of religion*   Religious sensitivity is partially advertence to the spiritual mysteries of life. But coupled with such sensitivity is personal tension simply because such mysteries are 'beyond' and 'within'. The individual person is conscious of his own position as standing over against the spirituality of the universe which confronts him, and yet with which he is enabled by his own spiritual nature to unite.

Religious sensitivity intensifies the feeling that a man is in this world and yet not entirely of this world: that he is a stranger sojourning here, a wanderer on a pilgrimage without a permanent home here. Thus Thomas à Kempis speaks of 'we, exiled children of Eve'[7] and Augustine remarks on the 'restlessness' of man.[8] And in our own century Whitehead has emphasized 'solitariness' as 'constituting the heart of religious importance'. He comments,[9]

> The great religious conceptions which haunt the imaginations of civilized mankind are scenes of solitariness: Prometheus chained to his rock, Mahomet brooding in the desert, the meditations of the Buddha, the solitary Man on the Cross. It belongs to the depth of the religious spirit to have felt forsaken, even by God.

Thus at the heart of the religious dimension is the awareness of the self, alone, independent and 'over-against' the things of this world both physical and spiritual.

Such solitariness, with all the threats of the contingency of existence, is not the totality of the religious dimension, however much it may be at its heart. In addition to an element of opposition there is the further element of potential relationship which is spiritual communion, and often union. It is this latter element – this deepest experience of the deepest interaction – that enables the religious man to regard life as 'meaningful'. What haunts man as a rational person is 'the ghost of significant action':[10] that is, the apparent meaninglessness of so much apparently meaningful action and activity. And this, as we have seen, is a spiritual mystery. The spiritual communion-which-is-union, endemic in the religious dimension, identifies that which is to be most prized and highly valued as of ultimate concern in life and thus succours hope and interest by providing the means through which human endeavours can be identified as significant.

(v) *The cosmological transcendence of the dimension* That which religion provides in order to identify human endeavours as significant (or otherwise) is the ontological grounding of objective value. Of constant concern to any reflective person is both the identification of that which is genuinely worthwhile together with recognition of that which is real and lasting. And these two cognitions must ultimately synthesize for there is little point in abiding by values (even unto death) if such values have little or nothing to do with what in fact is the real situation. And in a way which can only be described as 'paradoxical' in strict terminology the religious dimension transcends the logical chasm between 'ought' and 'is' and insists that that which 'is' is of greatest value, and that that which 'is' is spiritual.[11]

> The peculiar character of religious truth is that it explicitly deals with values. It brings into our consciousness that permanent side of the universe which we can care for. It thereby provides a meaning, in terms of values, for our existence, a meaning which flows from the nature of things.

The religious dimension of life is therefore essentially transcendent. By rooting values in the spiritual givenness of the natural order religion transcends the traditional distinctions of aesthetic, moral and intellectual values over against factual assertions. It intuits that the spiritual order is fundamental to all that exists and that in the spiritual order is to be found the unconditional character of the moral imperative and the power of right action, the inexhaustible depth of genuine creation and the illumination of the beautiful and the lovely, and the desire and longing for embracing the real which is the essence of truth.

Simply because the religious dimension of life is essentially transcendent so it has a universality not possessed by other dimensions of personal life whereby it projects into other dimensions of personal life,[12] not so much in terms of providing intellectual posits and categories, but in illuminating all endeavours by insisting on the spiritual depth and ultimacy of life. In so doing it does not destroy the logical autonomy of independent dimensions but illumines and transcends them by expanding their outlook and intensifying their values. Thus Christian endeavours, for example, may all be undertaken both in their own terms and *ad gloriam Dei*: and those qualities of life such as happiness, pleasure and moral rectitude are not denied but transformed into bliss, joy, peace and holiness.

Religion does not provide one with a speculative explanatory system of the universe which is pseudo-scientific and metaphysical: instead it supplements and intensifies empirical explanations by insisting that any kind of explanation of things and thinghood is incomplete without some referral to the spiritual dimension of personal life. Thus the transcending function of the spiritual life necessarily implies an intense cosmological awareness on the part of religious man. This is undoubtedly metaphysical: but it is a metaphysical awareness and experience, not a metaphysical explanation of a rational order. Moreover it is an awareness which provokes feelings of dependence, frailty, awe and wonder – and not those of intellectual surety and comprehension.

(vi) *The practicality of the religious dimension*   Such 'creature-feeling' and sense of dependence, which Otto identified as arising in the mind in the presence of the 'numinous',[13] give rise to the religious idea that the communion of the self with the spiritual presence is the 'way of life'.

Whether this way be conceived as one of salvation, enlightenment, identification or acceptance of fate, implicit in the religious dimension are those activities and actions whose *raison d'être* is none other than the transcending of the self by deifying the human, immortalizing the mortal, and generating the non-regenerative. The fundamental and all-embracing concern of the religious dimension of personal life is life itself in its total spiritual depth. And as the spiritual is timeless, infinite, immanent and unconditional so likewise is the religious dimension of personal life.

The religious dimension of personal life is that perennial, ubiquitous, dialectical spiritual interaction immanent in each person: and a religious person is not necessarily a good man but a saint.[14]

(vii) *Criteria of spiritual progress*   Finally we must face the question, 'What are the criteria implicit in the religious dimension whereby the presence of this spiritual interaction may be recognized?' And it may be confidently asserted that the first of such criteria is 'freedom'.

The dialectic harmony of each individual person in spiritual communion with ultimate reality is necessarily evidenced by actions, attitudes, dispositions and emotions which instantiate transcendent personal freedom. As the spiritual interaction progresses so there is a growing freedom from dependence upon material things, and from the materialistic desires and strivings which accompany man's interaction with them. There is also that freedom from selfishness, so that giving oneself confidently in love becomes more and more possible. There is that freedom from fear of destruction both physical and mental, moral and intellectual, as the interaction with the all-embracing powerful spiritual depth of being accelerates.

Such freedom manifests itself in spiritual strength: which is not a haughty and arrogant imposition of a powerful self but a quiet and humble steadiness in the face of 'the slings and arrows of outrageous fortune'. In times of grief and danger such strength stems from personal union with ultimate spiritual reality and whilst it manifests 'freedom' it is also indicative of a peace which is confidence. Such peace is not the pacificity of the non-combatant but the surety, joy and contentment of the person who knows that which is of ultimate value and which ultimately is, and who thereby recognizes the transient and ephemeral as the merely relative. Genuine spiritual interaction is always evidenced by rock-like qualities of peace.

Personal freedom from debilitating constraints, and quiet confidence in the face of misfortune and difficulties, as criteria of spiritual progress, do not necessarily entail that the spiritual life is one of eremitical withdrawal from the hurly-burly of daily life, however. That which is spiritual is that which is dynamic and thus any intensification of spiritual interaction results in energetic pursual of what is deemed to be ontologically necessary and objectively desirable. *So* those actions, activities, states of affairs and situations which are the outworkings of true spirituality in everyday life are those which are deemed just and righteous. Spiritual dynamism is always forceful adherence to, and promotion of, the real and proper in life. It is freedom, peace and justice (righteousness) which are the criteria of ongoing spiritual interaction.

(viii) *Some implications for general aims* We thus begin to observe those dimensional criteria which the general aims of religious education should satisfy. In a task sense, religious education is advertence to the spiritual dimension of life – to the non-physical, non-rational and dynamic element of personal life. Therefore the approach must be one of at least sensitizing pupils to the mysterious, non-sensational depths of life present both in individual persons and in the cosmos which is independent of oneself.[15]

Such an approach, however, must neither explicitly nor implicitly suggest that religion provides one with an explanatory view of the world and of life, alternative to that of the natural sciences, which 'solves' the mysteries. Instead, religious education must concentrate on alerting young people to the possibility of a cosmological awareness which is one of transcendent order and value. Furthermore, it must provoke the insight that such a metaphysical awareness is not necessarily an intellectual study but a practical mode of life. It is personal transcendence which is holiness.

The practical task which arises in all this is the indentification of those particular areas of personal life which must be centred upon in any syllabus of religious education. And we may well draw a little closer to achieving this by stating clearly the necessary and sufficient conditions of the concept of religion implicit in the phrase 'the religious dimension of personal life'.

2 The formal conditions of the concept

(i) *The primacy of man's spiritual nature* If there is any insight into the true nature of relgion in Feuerbach's 'anthropotheistic' account; if there is any philosophic truth in Freud's explication of the divine as an 'illusory projection'; if there is any logical significance in Marx's view of religion as 'alienated human self-consciousness'; and if there is any wisdom in the popular, cynical remark that 'man made God in his own image' it is this – that whenever the concept of 'religion' is employed about persons then necessarily implicit in its use is the connotation of personal self-awareness as spiritual.

Implicit in the concept is the sense of a person being wholly spiritual: that is, that a person is spiritual in all the fullness of that term. On the other hand, the concept of 'religion' does not connote any denial of the physical and rational in life. It cannot be denied that particular religious faiths have in fact regarded the physical and rational as illusory in their doctrinal formulations: but in their actual practices they have both employed rational procedures and gone to great lengths to 'overcome' the physical in such a way as to suggest recognition of their 'significance' if not their 'reality'.

This latter attitude is entirely intelligible once it is realized that the concept of religion lays stress not simply upon a person's spirituality but upon the primacy of the spirit in personal life. Religion necessarily implies the primacy of the spirit in terms of value and ontology over both the physical and rational nature of personal life. A religious view of man – a religious attitude towards anything for that matter – is one which grounds physical and mental phenomena in spiritual reality. As was argued in section 1 (v), implicit in religion is a transcendence of fact and value distinctions through identification of the ultimates of each in spiritual reality. The concept of religion implies man's spiritual self-awareness in such a way that the primacy of the spiritual over the mental and physical is both mooted and emphasized.

(ii) *The infinitizable subject*   The essence of such spiritual self-awareness is the sense of being a free subject and not a conditioned object. It is a self-consciousness of the self as a centre of reason, affection and will; as one who thinks, loves, acts, chooses, values and creates. And involved in this awareness is a consciousness of being one who originates action rather than one who simply reacts to stimuli; who deliberately surrenders autonomy on occasions rather than being necessarily heteronomous; and who is capable of valuing objects and courses of action in terms of objective intrinsicity rather than gainful instrumentality. Moreover it is a consciousness of the liveliness of a self which is alive and which promotes its life with zest and passion.

Such a self is wholly spiritual. It is dynamic, being a source of power and energy and an active director of zestful endeavour. It is non-rational in the sense of rising above and beyond the rational in its affections and commitment to values. And it is non-physical being unbridled by spatio-temporal considerations. Indeed, we may agree with Feuerbach that such is the consciousness of this self-conscious self that it rises above physical limitations to an awareness of infinitude,[16] even if such an awareness is not an intellectual comprehension of infinitude.

Such awareness of infinitude is to be expected of a being which is conscious of its own consciousness because 'Consciousness, in the strict and proper sense, is identical with consciousness of the infinite: a limited consciousness is no consciousness; consciousness is essentially infinite in its nature.'[17] The spiritual element in personal life is not bound by physical restrictions or by the limitations of intellectual formulations, but is capable of being transcendently infinitized. And the concept of religion points to this awareness of the person as being primarily a spiritual and infinitizable subject.

This connotation is present in the regular categorization of a good many human attitudes and dispositions as 'religious'. There is, for example, concern with immortality, and the aspirations and yearnings which exceed any mortal capacity for satisfaction. There is the sense of alienation, of being an exile here on earth, and the desire for liberation from dissatisfying empirical reality. There is that longing for 'peace which is unity' which is the cessation of the 'warring of selves'[18] and the brotherhood of all in an infinite unity. All such dispositions are termed 'religious' because the concept of religion implies this awareness of the person being primarily a spiritual and infinitizable subject.

(iii) *The dependent and vulnerable self* Involved in such personal self-consciousness is another facet of conscious interaction – a sense of dependence. The awareness of the self as a dynamic, originating, creative subject cannot be denied: yet accompanying this intuition is that 'My self is given to me far more than it is formed by me.'[19] However great may be that sense of freedom of choice and action, which is the essence of spirituality,[20] it is nevertheless accompanied by that other sense of the mystery of being whereby the sheer contingency of our existence is borne in upon us. However creative each of us may be, each is nevertheless aware that ultimately he did not create himself and that our existence is fundamentally one of mystery. 'In the last resort the profound life, the fontal life, the new-born life, escape our grasp entirely.'[21]

If such dependence is explained away by reference to some

social structure this is but a partial explanation because the insufficiency of individual existence is never evaporated by the multiplication and summing of such individuals. This is the religious insight of the traditional cosmological argument for the existence of God – that man is fundamentally a dependent being – even if the logic of that argument fails to support its purported conclusion.

Such an awareness of dependence evokes in man a sense of wonder and anxiety because, lacking self-sufficiency, he realizes his possible vulnerability. He is threatened by[22]

death itself, the unforeseeability of the future, the irretrievable nature of the past (so that one can do little to retrieve or undo what one has already done), the apparently random or fortuitous nature of some events, such as disease, or earthquake, or madness.

And if some of these limitations seem altogether too 'physical' to be of concern to 'spiritual' man then à Kempis leaves one in no doubt of other threats:[23]

Here man is defiled by many sins, ensnared by many passions, a prey to countless fears. Racked by many cares, and distracted by many strange things, he is entangled in many vanities. He is hedged in by many errors, worn out by many labours, burdened by temptations, enervated by pleasures, tormented by want.

We may therefore conlude that the concept of religion implies an awareness of oneself as primarily a spiritual subject, potentially infinitizable yet dependent and vulnerable.

(iv) *The objectively given spiritual reality*   Any personal self-awareness is always awareness of oneself as an interacting agent: and as was shown in the previous section, the religious dimension of personal life is a spiritual interaction in which the spirit of man 'within' is in dialectical harmony with the spirit of the cosmos 'beyond'. This being so, the concept of religion implies the objective reality of the ultimate spirituality of the cosmos.

The idea that man is a spiritual subject is often assented to by non-religious humanists: but the idea of an objective spiritual reality is one which provokes a great deal of debate. This is nothing new: the theory that such is a psychological projection, an 'illusion' which is a fulfilment 'of the oldest, strongest and most urgent wishes of mankind'[24] was succinctly summarized long ago by Petronius who declared that 'fear first made gods upon the earth'.[25] Freud was merely following a long tradition of sceptical speculation which found technical expression in a good many writers of the last century.

Many such accounts of religion are, however, irrelevant to an analysis of the concept for two reasons. First, they are often predominantly causal accounts: and one can no more say what is meant by 'religion' by telling a psychological story of how some people become religious than one can distinguish between 'fruit' and 'vegetable' by relating how the plants are grown. Second, they often lack objectivity in the sense of reinterpreting religion, and religious activities, rather than giving an account of it as it is.

Whatever the difficulty of understanding the religious position, and whatever one's likes and dislikes of it, there can be no doubt that incipient in the religious dimension of life is an awareness of an objective spiritual reality which is encountered as a given – 'a sense of being grasped by the Spiritual Presence'.[26] This is a crucial, necessary facet of the religious dimension of personal life and is the reason why so many definitions of the term 'religion' include some reference to 'god' or 'gods'.

(v) *The 'essentiality' and 'hiddenness' of the spiritual reality*
Now in so far as the objectively given spiritual reality is necessarily non-physical it is thereby metaphysical. But what does not follow from this is that the Object of religious devotion is either a metaphysical concept, construct, axiomatic posit or a projection of human desires, wishes and affections. Indeed, where such is in fact the object of devotion then one perceives an irreligious attitude.

That man does conceptualize ultimate spiritual reality – in terms such as God, Allah, Brahman – and does thereby direct his affections cannot be denied. But the idea that such a conceptualization is the sum totality of ultimate spiritual reality is once again irreligious. Indeed, what has to be clearly understood about the Object on the religious dimension of life is that it possesses the twin features of 'essentiality' and 'hiddenness' (or 'ineffability').

The fundamental experience of the religious life is the confrontation of the individual self with that which is ultimate in the cosmos: ultimate both in being the ontological ground of all existing things and all possible thinghood, and being the criterion of all value. As the ultimate ground of all being the religious Object is sensed as absolute not relative, permanent not temporary, unconditioned not conditioned, infinite not finite. As such its value is unquestionable. It is utterly reliable, consistent and perfect: and being wholly spiritual it is omnipotent. As such it is essential: and in that essentiality it unifies any divergencies and ambiguities and is thereby transcendent. Moreover, it is thereby the 'ordering' quality of life.

It is because the Object of the religious dimension is sensed as such that it is holy and sacred, and in its purity it remains hidden. Whilst being the ground of life it is nevertheless apart from the contingent, ephemeral and transient order of everyday affairs and is ineffable. It is intuited rather than known theoretically: and whether it is confronted in 'the still, small voice of conscience', contuited along with contingent events, referred to by 'signals of transcendence' or realized in 'peak experiences'[27] it remains as much veiled as revealed, as much mysterious as perceived. All conceptualizations, all verbal and non-verbal symbolizations, all relationships and activities only hint at it and point to it rather than encompass it.

It is because the object of that interaction which is the religious dimension of life is of this nature that there arise the great paradoxes of religion: the emotions of fear and love, wonder and anxiety; the perception of overtly and obviously physical phenomena of a finite, contingent, temporal order in terms of the infinite, eternal and ahistorical; the need for revelation so that man might know. And it is the sense of this 'numinous' which gives confidence unto martyrdom, optimism in times of desolation, and wisdom rather than expertise.

We may therefore conclude that a second necessary condition for the application of the concept of religion is the objective reality of the spiritual ultimacy of the cosmos, both essential and ineffable.

(vi) *The surrender of autonomy*   The religious dimension of life implies no subjective metaphysic but is in fact a subject-object interaction. As such it is identical with every other dimension of personal life. And if such dimensions are to be rich and fulsome – if life is to be truly personal – then the interaction can only be authentic if the objectivity of the object is respected. This necessitates an openness of being on the part of the person which is essentially one of self-discipline: in Temple's words, 'The first condition of attainment in Science, Art or Religion is not loyalty to self, but forgetfulness of self in concentration on the object; it is most truly the meek who possess the earth.'[28] This being so, the question arises as to the exact form of self-discipline, or openness of being, which is implicit in the concept of religion.

Now in so far as the objectivity of the object must be respected for any subject-object interaction to be authentic, it is formally the case that an appropriate openness of being will be essentially one of suitable response to the object. And in so far as the object of the religious dimension of life is the spiritual ultimacy of the cosmos, both essential and ineffable, so the suitable response cannot be one of attempted mastery and manipulation, or one of theoretical cognition. Instead, an appropriate openness on the part of the self can only be one of faith and commitment.

'Faith', it has already been argued (chapter 2: section 2 (i)) is not a feature of just one dimension of life, however, in so far as it is the exercise of subjective agency by persons who are multi-dimensional harmonies. To speak of 'faith' with regard to the religious dimension of life is therefore to draw attention to but one aspect of a person's committal to a pattern of reality-controlled interaction. And this aspect is the self-denial of the autonomy of the subject.

The concept of religion implies surrender, submission, resignation, sacrifice of the self as a subject to that upon which one ultimately depends which is the permanent, absolute, unconditioned, essential ground of all that is. Thus, 'Man's true spiritual progress depends on the denial of the self, and he who renounces self is completely free and secure.'[29] 'Religion' implies that such self-denying love is the only possible openness of being whereby lies the road of liberty from the vulnerability of life and all threats to existence and bliss. Indeed the great paradox of religion (which seems so clearly expressed in Buddhism) is that the way of existence for the self is the way of non-existence of the self.

Such love of the holy is the pursuit of the good because the distinction of what 'is' from what is valuable is transcended in the spiritual ultimate reality. For the religious person there is no distinction between devotion to the ultimate Spiritual Presence and a delight in right conduct. The essence of both is the antithesis of egocentricity and selfishness (In theistic terms, 'autonomy' becomes 'theonomy'.)

Such self-sacrifice of the subject is manifest again and again in the rites, rituals and codes of conduct of particular religions: but their true religious significance does not lie in the correct physical performance of the rite (that is 'magic') or in the beneficial instrumentality of right action. As religious practices their validity is their inner worth. Religious self-sacrifice is not donation of the physical in life but is the surrender of the spirituality of the subject. So that which is critical in a religious ethic, for example, is right motive, not right action: and it is the direction of the will of the person which is of supreme religious concern.

À Kempis writes, 'While man looks on outward appearances, God looks into your heart. Man sees your actions, but God your motives' and 'to live inwardly to God, and not to be bound by worldly affections, is the proper state of the spiritual man.'[30] And Whitehead speaks of 'the internal life which is the self-realization of existence' and comments that 'Religion is the art and the theory of the internal life of man, so far as it depends on man himself and on that which is permanent in the nature of things.'[31]

(vii) *Spiritual purity*   The problem for each person, however, is that one is not simply a spiritual self but also a physical being who so often finds the allurements of the physical dominating – especially in the belief that the spiritual dimension of personality can in fact find fulfilment in the physical. Moreover there is the constant tendency of the self to be self-affirming; and when such self-affirmation expresses itself wholeheartedly in the physical then the inner, spiritual dimension of personal life is doomed. (This is the reason why so many religious thinkers condemn out of hand sexual lust, but not love which expresses itself sexually.) Accordingly the concept of religion implies that not only is self-sacrifice of the subject necessary but impossible without purity.

The problem here is that 'purity' is often understood only in its negative sense: a sense of 'getting rid of all that fouls'. And whilst one does not wish to deny that it does have this connotation, nevertheless it is in its more positive sense that it is of religious significance.

The positive sense is that of having an ultimate and holding to it, of being concerned with it through thick and thin. To be spiritually pure is to hold steadfastly to a pursuit or goal despite numerous temptations and distractions. It is not a matter of suffering 'tunnel-vision' and of not perceiving other alternatives, but of having a unity of purpose whereby the diverse teleology of a complex life-pattern is subsumed under a single goal. Kierkegaard says of the inner life that its task[32]

> is to exercise the absolute relationship to the absolute *telos*, striving to reach the maximum of maintaining simultaneously a relationship to the absolute *telos* and to relative ends, not by mediating them, but by making the relationship to the absolute *telos* absolute, and the relationship to the relative ends relative.

It is because the concept of religion implies this sense of purity that religion can be spoken of as 'of ultimate concern' by Tillich and others. But is only when such purity implies ultimate concern with ultimate spiritual reality that it is truly religious purity.

We may therefore conclude that the third, and final, necessary condition for the application of the concept religion is an openness of being characterized by spiritual self-sacrifice and purity of the subject.

3 Dimensional criteria

We began this chapter by asserting that educational activities contribute to objective self-integration by provoking personal understanding of man's position and status in the cosmos. In the light of our examination of the religious dimension of personal life it may now be argued that religiously educational activities are those which sensitize children to the mysteries of life and enable them to view the cosmos, and their place in it, in spiritual terms if they so wish.

It cannot be emphasized too strongly that religiously educational activities provoke intellectual understanding of the spiritual dimension of personal life and not of the moral, political or sociological dimensions. There is no doubt that the spiritual dimension of personal life does reach over into these other dimensions and infuse and energize them in such a way that it is sometimes difficult to disentangle the dimensional web of personal interaction. Thus the reduction of many RE lessons to 'moral education', 'social problems' and 'ideological studies' – or even to 'education in life stances'[33] – is understandable. But it is not excusable. And it is hardly sound thinking to assert that such 'areas of concern' are central to religious education.

Moral, social and political situations may all be sound launching pads for flights of provocation of intellectual understanding of a person's spiritual dimension but that is their only true role in religious education. Religiously educational activities specifically contribute to the total education of children by provoking intellectual understanding of man as a person *vis-à-vis* the person as a spiritual subject, the objective spiritual order of the cosmos, and the kind of pattern of reality-controlled interaction which enables the fulfilment and enrichment of man's spirit.

The approach of the religious educator to this task must therefore be one of constant concern with these three spiritual areas of personal life. It is these three areas which should provide the fundamental framework of any syllabus of religious education – not religious scriptures, doctrines, customs, rituals, organizations, myths, etc. To religiously educate anyone is to provoke answers in spiritual terms to the question, 'What am I as a person?'

Religious education is not primarily concerned with the study of the Bible: that is 'Scripture'. Nor is it simply concerned with imparting information about the religions of the world: that is 'Religious Knowledge'. And it is certainly not any form of 'religious instruction' which furthers the work of any one *congregatio fidelium*. Indeed, such should be the vibrancy of religious education that it enables men and women to critically assess organized religions in terms of spiritual criteria – and not simply in terms of moral, financial and social values.

Religiously educational activities provoke intellectual understanding of the spirituality of personality in all its extensiveness and dynamism. This being so, we must attempt to become a little clearer about the logical nature of intellectual understanding before offering any practical suggestions for teaching religion in an educational sense.

Chapter 4

Intellectual understanding

Insight or understanding is itself a relationship with the times, distinct from both involvement and withdrawal.

J. S. Dunne: *The Way of All the Earth*

Introduction

On a good many occasions a person is described as being 'very understanding', or, as being 'an understanding person'. At such times attention is being drawn to their sympathetic character and kindly disposition to others. This laudable attitude is undoubtedly worthy of attention by philosophers of education but in this chapter we shall be concerned with that kind of understanding which may be briefly alluded to as intellectual insight and comprehension. Furthermore we are concerned with a person's understanding: whether or not animals, insects or divine beings share in such understanding is not a matter for discussion here.

Intellectual understanding is apparently paradoxical. To understand something is to be both active and passive, to be master and subject, to conquer and to be conquered, to create and to assimilate, to analyse and to synthesize. As an intellectual phenomenon, understanding is abortive without rich draughts of physical sensation: and as an individual attainment it is stunted if bereft of communal contributions. It is achieved only by searching which entails waiting, and learning by those who are already learned. It cannot be taught and yet without teaching it remains minimal and puerile. A will-o'-the-wisp it enchants only to deceive because he who achieves some understanding soon perceives its infinite breadth and depth.

This apparently paradoxical nature of understanding is in fact evidence of its fundamental logic: namely, that understanding is always necessarily both subjective and objective. This is only to be expected in the case of a person's understanding because intellectual understanding is but part of one of the dimensions – 'mind' – of the objective self-integration which is personhood. It is but one aspect of the harmonious ongoing interaction whereby each person forges his own creative becoming and, as such, must be understood in interactive terms.

A person's understanding of anything is but part of the overall ongoing interaction: and Pole's observation that, as regards understanding, the chief question is 'the nature of the actual relation between the private and the public side of understanding'[1] is seminal because it is necessary.

Any understanding of understanding must advert to an identification of those powers of the individual person whereby he apprehends himself and other objects, of those parts of the human environment which are necessary features of that interaction implicit in 'understanding', together with a characterization of the quality of the interaction involved in 'understanding'. And in so far as 'consciousness' is necessary for that form of prehension known as 'apprehension' so we may begin to grapple with understanding a person's understanding of an object by considering the nature of individual consciousness implicit in understanding anything.

1 Individual consciousness by way of social determinants

(i) *The social character of private consciousness* Of supreme importance in the development of self-consciousness are those other human minds with which each individual person's mind interacts. It is an important truism that intellectual development is directly affected by association with, and by reaction to, those other human minds which each person meets either 'in the flesh' or by means of reprographic devices. And this is because, in a very peculiar and profound manner, each individual person's mind becomes like those minds which nurture it.

It can be asserted of each of us that the language we use, the categories of thought we employ, the beliefs we hold and the ideals we adhere to are not of our own creation but in fact belong to public, social traditions into which we have been tuned by others. We may ultimately make something of these traditions for ourselves but we can never deny their pertinence nor ignore their demands. Our intellectual endeavours – indeed, all dimensions of individual personality – are meaningless without reference to objective public traditions with which each interacts.

The importance of social parameters in individual personal achievements must be grasped if there is to be any understanding of understanding. To understand is always to understand something: and whilst understanding an object is always over and beyond merely being conscious of that object nevertheless the apprehension of an object is logically necessary for its understanding. Without the self-conscious apprehension of objects there would be no understanding of them: and unless each individual person 'stands under' social conceptual schemes there can be no such apprehension.

(ii) *The necessity of accurate descriptions*   In so far as 'we never understand a thing *per se*: rather we understand it under some description'[2] so, strictly speaking, all objects of a person's understanding are those conceptual formulations in which the descriptions of, say, signs or actions or pieces of machinery, are apprehended.

Such conceptual formulations may vary from age to age, from ethnic group to ethnic group, from person to person within the same social group, and even within the life of the same person. It is quite possible to describe the same action as an execution, sacrifice, murder, manslaughter or euthanasia: or the same series of actions as a fight for freedom, a just war, a civil war, a revolution or even a holy war. The particular 'chunk of reality' which is the purported object of understanding is therefore never capable of being understood in 'neutral'

69

terms but always and only under and within some conceptual pattern.

At first sight this conclusion would appear to sound the death-knell of any attempt to distinguish true understanding of an object from misunderstanding of that same object for if three spectators sitting alongside each other apprehend the one and same series of actions as a religious ritual, a rain-making ceremony or a game of cricket, and understand it in these terms, who is to say that any one, or all three, is misunderstanding the situation?

The point to be grasped, however, is this: that whilst different descriptions of the same 'chunk of reality' *may* be given, not all the descriptions need be *accurate*. One man kills another: but to describe such an action as 'a sacrifice' might be to miss the mark completely. The only accurate description might be 'manslaughter in self-defence'.

From the foregoing it can now be perceived that one of the primary requirements of understanding something is not that the object must be understood under some description but rather that it must be understood under some *accurate* description. And it follows that part of what is meant by objective understanding, in the rational sense of 'objective', is reference to the accuracy of the description of the object which is to be understood.

One thing that does not follow from all this is that there can be only one accurate description of an item. In so far as man employs different patterns, or families, of concepts to formulate his descriptions, so different descriptions may on occasion be each and all accurate. Thus, the table at which I am writing may be described by employing, say, aesthetic, chemical and historical concepts – and if it were in a sanctuary in a church, in religious concepts as well. Each of the four descriptions given could be accurate: and each, therefore, would be a (slightly) different object of understanding. In this way one begins to perceive part of the difference between a person's ways of understanding himself and objects around him – *viz*. the kind of conceptual framework which is employed to formulate an accurate description.

(iii) *Membership of a social group*   In so far as all objects of understanding are accurate conceptual formulations of a descriptive nature it follows necessarily that in order to understand a particular object one must both possess concepts relevant to that particular description and also be cognizant of the criteria of accuracy appertaining to the conceptual formulation. Here one comes face to face with the existential interaction between the individual agent on the one hand and a social milieu on the other hand.

It is obvious that the necessity of apprehending any given description is consequent upon mastery of the language in which the formulation is constructed. One recalls Tennyson's lines:

> At last I heard a voice upon the slope
> Cry to the summit, 'Is there any hope?'
> To which an answer pealed from that high land,
> But in a tongue no man could understand;
> And on the glimmering limit far withdrawn,
> God made Himself an awful rose of dawn.

The divine answer in Tennyson's 'Vision of Sin' is unintelligible because it is given in an unknown tongue. Such a *sine qua non* of the understanding of any spoken or written word is common experience for if one does not know the 'tongue' which is being employed then one cannot apprehend the description. But whilst such mastery is a matter of individual personal achievement nevertheless the tongue itself belongs to a society, whether large or small. To speak a language is a major step towards becoming a member of a group.

Speaking a language is much more than surface grammatical mastery of a tongue, however: and apprehending a particular description is more than syntactical skill. At the least it is to possess those concepts and to be cognizant of those criteria of accuracy referred to earlier. But these are not possessed in isolation, as it were, but are part and parcel of what Wittgenstein terms 'a form of life'.[3] To grasp a particular description is to be aware of much larger contexts. Wittgenstein puts his finger on the point:[4]

'After he had said this, he left here as he did the day before.'
Do I understand this sentence? Do I understand it just as I

should if I heard it in the course of a narrative? If it were set down in isolation I should say, I don't know what it's about. But all the same I should know how this sentence might perhaps be used: I could myself invent a context for it.

It is because of this fierce logical dependence of the particular linguistic construct upon the general that Wittgenstein is right to say that 'understanding a sentence is much more akin to understanding a theme in music than one may think.'[5] The particular only 'makes sense' in terms of the general.

Ziff emphasizes this point in chapter 8 of his book. He argues, 'The causes of ununderstanding are legion: any factor relevant to the understanding of what is said may contribute equally to an instance of ununderstanding. Thus phonetic, phonemic, morphologic, syntactic, semantic, discourse and perceptual factors may be operative.'[6] Taking as an example the locution, 'A cheetah can outrun a man' he argues that the intelligibility of such an observation is as dependent upon specifications which are implicit in a form of discourse as upon those which are explicit. Furthermore, the making explicit that which is implicit in any discourse is difficult because not only would such a set of specifications be numerous and heterogeneous but such heterogeneity would preclude the possibility of an effective specific.

Faced with this difficulty it is usual, Ziff points out, to appeal to the 'normal', 'ordinary' or 'common'. But this can still be obscure on occasions: for example, what is to count as 'normal' in the locution, 'A normal cheetah can under normal conditions outrun a normal man'? Ziff concludes, 'If the hearer is to understand what is said then the hearer, like the speaker, must have some sort of conceptual scheme: he must have some conception of a cheetah, and of a man, of running and so forth' and he 'must understand and appreciate the form of representation employed by the speaker.'[7]

Whilst the possession of a conceptual scheme is a matter of individual personal attainment it is nevertheless the product of social interaction. Even on those occasions when genius creates a new conceptual outlook such creation is nevertheless rooted in some social milieu (e.g. Teilhard de Chardin's 'noosphere' in *The Phenomenon of Man*). To be an understanding person is in the first place to share in a social conceptual scheme.

Sharing in a social conceptual scheme involves 'standing under' a whole realm of public determinants: and unless one subjects oneself to such determinants then no appraisal of the real as the real is possible. This, however, necessarily results in one interpreting, or viewing, objects in certain particular ways because conceptual schemes are different and particular.

The particularity of each conceptual scheme lies in the employment of particular posits and categories, the holding of particular metaphysical beliefs and expectations, the making of particular perceptions and the pursuit of particular logic. These four features are here separated out for purposes of academic convenience: in practice they coalesce in schematic interdependence. And it is only in terms of any one particular conceptual scheme that an object may be apprehended and accurately described.

The number of objects that any individual agent may apprehend, and the number of ways in which any single object (say, a photograph) may be apprehended, is therefore dependent upon the number of particular conceptual schemes into which that person has been initiated. Without the conscious apprehension of objects there can be no understanding of them: and there can be no such consciousness without self-discipline whereby one 'stands under' public determinants. Such determinants are not only public in principle but also in origin and herein lies a major facet of the relation between the private and public nature of understanding – that understanding objects implies individual consciousness of reality, and such consciousness is impossible without the employment of public determinants of conceptualization.

2 An interactive state of creative intuition

(i) *Individual creativity* The argument so far has stressed the public, social determinants of private consciousness and in so doing has drawn attention to the 'given' of life with which each individual person interacts. As far as understanding

understanding is concerned it is now apparent that this 'given' is both a social milieu and a brute universe. But in understanding anything the individual mind does not simply receive conceptual structures from the social milieu, and stimuli and sensations from physical objects, but makes a positive contribution of its own.

In one sense all understanding is individual and personal because only I, and I alone, can understand something for myself. Even if someone else were to convey some insight to me I would still have to make it mine, to grasp it, before I could be said to understand. To this extent 'understanding' as an intellectual phenomenon is never simply an interrelationship of the individual agent, the social milieu and the universe, but an interaction.

Involved in this state of interaction is a multiplicity of causes and causal sequences which are often thoroughly distinct and disparate. Memory, other people's locutions, visual and tactual stimuli, one's own beliefs, hopes, fears, aspirations may all exert different causal influence upon one. Sometimes one tries hard to make sense of 'what's being said' or 'what's going on' and fails: at other times one succeeds in understanding.

Now one's trying hard (paying attention, listening carefully) may well be a major causal factor in understanding something but it is only one of a number of such factors. And sometimes one tries hard to understand and does not succeed. In other words, that state of interaction which is 'understanding' is dependent upon an amalgam of memories, thoughts, percepts, attitudes, images, etc. and yet such causal products do not necessarily result in understanding. That state of interaction we call 'understanding' is not the direct outcome of any deterministic chain.

If understanding is not determined then two things follow. First, that state of interaction is one in which creativeness is paramount. And from that it follows, secondly, that it is essentially a free state.

Enmeshed in a web of causal chains, a dissonant cacophony of impugning demands, the understanding agent welds an harmonious theme of relatedness and significance. And this metamorphosis of the incomprehensible to the comprehensible is an act of creation, a free act. It cannot be a necessary effect of some particular successful causal process because if it were the product would be nothing more than just another effect amongst all the other effects indicated above and thus the disharmony of the particular effects would remain, a disunited chaos of innumerable logically distinct entities. To understand is that creative state of interaction which brings order out of chaos and thus 'excludes a background of intellectual incoherence'.[8]

(ii) *Ecstatic intuition of relations*   Ubiquitously insistent within this creative state of interaction is intuition. To understand is to possess immediate apprehension of correct relations – 'immediate' in the sense that such discernment is other than inference or symbolic thought. To understand is not to abrogate or to deny linguistic reasoning but it is to go beyond symbolic discourse to perceive those necessary relations without which reasoning itself is but the regurgitation of shibboleths and the mouthing of slogans. To this extent, and in this way, understanding is shot through with penetrative insight whereby the agent sees and grasps the inner character and hidden nature of things.

Here, if anywhere, there is a genuine paradox of understanding resolved only in terms of interaction because what is now being argued is that 'understanding' is creative only in so far as it 'discovers' what is already 'there'. Its synthetic capability is based upon analysis. To understand is both to penetrate and to perceive hidden elements and to rise above particulars and to create new entities. It is to see wholes in terms of parts and unity in prolific diversity. It is to theorize in the sense of perceiving a necessary unity of pattern in the multifarious diversity of stimuli.

The creativity of this state of intuitive interaction is cumulative. To understand is to analogize by discerning new experiences in the light of old insights, to classify in terms of former comprehensions, to appraise within established values. And because of this cumulative feature understanding is therefore not only insight but foresight: it not only grasps present relations but it foresees potential consequences and future possibilities.

To understand is to be visionary in such a way that the

vision guides one's interpretation as one encounters and enters the unknown. And such vision is inherent in the ecstatic quality of understanding whereby the agent is enabled to 'stand outside himself' going beyond immediate spatio-temporal limitations. Indeed such cumulative, ecstatic vision is the hallmark of the intelligent person as he distinguishes the probable from the improbable, the plausible from the implausible, and the relevant from the irrelevant.

(iii) *Freedom and truth*   Such cumulative creative intuition is free because every creation is free. 'Here is the ultimate meaning of creation', writes Hartshorne, 'in the freedom or self-determination of any experience as a new "one", arising out of a previous many, in terms of which it cannot, by any causal relationship be fully described.'[9] But such freedom is not unbridled licence. Rather it is that freedom which comes from self-discipline, from 'standing under' the public determinants inherent in social conceptual schemes, from waiting attentively upon the objects to be understood.

To understand is not to apprehend just any insight: it is to perceive correct relations. Moreover, the accuracy of these discernments lies in the necessity of the relations because whilst many relationships may be possible within an object to be understood, and whilst it may be possible for an object to combine and interact in a variety of ways with other objects, nevertheless the intuition of such contingent relations is not the essence of understanding. All objects have a potential in terms of relationships but such is dependent upon the actual nature of the object(s): and the relations within this nature are of a necessary kind otherwise the object is not that which it purports to be.

To understand an object is to discern these necessary relations, to trace the interdependent structure and pattern which constitutes the object and to form a unified insight. It is to abide by the truth.

It is because freedom is allied to truth in understanding that understanding is the supreme intellectual virtue – 'supreme' both in value and governance. The imagination may run riot, the will may be dangerous and desire may mislead. It is quite possible to entertain wild thoughts and to embrace false beliefs, so much so that one's intentions, decisions and commitments are evil – unless all intellectual phenomena are subject to the understanding. It is impossible to be reasonable and to behave rationally without understanding, and any reasoning without understanding is liable to be irrational. As Whitehead observes: 'Understanding has this quality that, however it be led up to, it issues in the soul freely conforming its nature to the supremacy of insight. It is the reconciliation of freedom with the compulsion of truth.'[10]

Such reconciliation of freedom with the compulsion of truth in the interactive state of creative intuition is something which passes into the habitual texture of the mind and determines the intellectual tone of the person. And like certain other mental phenomena this state of mind is by no means static. Its penetrative accumulation of insight is never complete: its compositions are always open-ended. There is an ongoing quality to understanding rooted in sustained reflection and widening experience, a continuous stream of creation broadening and deepening as it flows. To be an understanding person is never to be in a state of being but always a state of becoming: it is never to scale an eschatological peak but always to inhabit a realm of individual potential.

3   The rich diversity of understanding

(i) *The given objects of understanding*   One of the reasons why understanding is a state of potential is its rich diversity. Attention has already been drawn to the fact that persons employ a variety of conceptual schemes to apprehend objects of understanding, and to apprehend the same object under different accurate descriptions (cf. section 1). The richness of understanding does not lie simply in the variety of ways in which persons advert to objects but also in the number of diverse relations intuited in objects consequent upon dissimilar ways of apprehension. This must now be illustrated before an attempt can be made to understand what is meant by 'breadth and depth of understanding': and it might be profitable to begin by briefly alluding to the diverse objects which people understand.

Among such objects, adverted to by means of accurate descriptions, are:

   (i)   physical signs (including the written word)
  (ii)   physical symbols
 (iii)   physical actions and activities (including animate signs, symbolic acts, non-verbal physical acts and locutionary acts)
 (iv)   the manner of activity and action
  (v)   the composition and employment of physical objects
 (vi)   the mechanical functioning of artifacts
(vii)   works of art
(viii)   other persons
 (ix)   combinations of the above in situations, events and states of affairs

People also claim to understand, or misunderstand, themselves and mental and spiritual phenomena both active and passive.

In addition to these examples there may well be other objects which exist which man either has not, or does not, apprehend. And this observation gives us a clue as to two formal qualities which any object must possess if it is to be intelligible to man. In the first place an object of human understanding must possess distinguishing marks such that it can be recognized by the human mind. Unless an object can be apprehended by means of the conceptual schemes employed by persons it cannot be comprehended.[11] And, second, for an object to be intelligible to a person it must possess the quality of 'logical coherence'.

The term 'logical' is here being employed in a wider sense than that of 'strict logic', although this will often be present. Thus, the purported object 'a square circle' is unintelligible in terms of strict logic: likewise 'a married bachelor' and 'a body without extension'. 'Logical coherence' will often imply appropriate means–end relationships, however, or efficient functioning.

In this extended sense of 'logical coherence' a sign, for example, must refer to some object or situation other than itself and should this referent cease to exist then the 'sign' loses its logical coherence as a sign. Similarly a purported human activity which lacks intention but is merely a random series of arbitrary acts is logically incoherent as an activity and thus unintelligible as such.

We thus observe that the understanding of an object by an individual person is best explained as a complex interaction of that person with the objectively given under the aegis of public social schemes of conceptualization. This being so, no object is ever understood 'neutrally', as it were, but always under some particular way of apprehension: and the same given item may be understood in quite different ways. One and the same cabbage may be intelligible to an individual person in aesthetic, chemical, nutritional, historical or religious ways. Moreover, in so far as 'understanding an object' implies 'intuition of correct relations' so one of the differences between kinds of understanding will be that of the exact relations discerned.

The formal differences between kinds of understanding will be explicated later (in section 4). At this stage an attempt must be made to distinguish some of the different relations which persons intuit in objects understood.

(ii) *Some relations perceived*   In attempting to list some of the different relations which may be perceived by the human mind we may profitably use the list of objects given above as a guide. This attempt is not meant to be an exhaustive taxonomy of such relations but rather an indication of the potential richness of human understanding.

All signs are parasitic upon some other object for their ontological status as signs. A sign points beyond itself to indicate another object such that the sign and its object form a pair. The relationship between the pair is asymmetrical, however, because the sign stands to the object it signals as a proxy, and thereby is dependent upon its object for its significance, whereas the object signalled is independent of its sign. Neither the logic nor the ontological status of the object is affected or determined by being signalled. The relation intuited in understanding a sign is therefore one of *referential dependence* of the sign upon its paired object.

In contrast to a sign a symbol does not just indicate an object but represents it. Signs announce objects and are symptomatic of their presence, or of their future existence: symbols convey their objects and are vehicles of significance. A symbol is not separated from that which is symbolized and the function of a symbol is to provoke and generate thoughts, attitudes, actions and dispositions relevant to that which is symbolized rather than simply to broadcast the presence of some other object. The relations between the nature of a symbol and that which is symbolized is therefore one of *referential interdependence* (and not one of referential dependence, as in the case of the sign).

In contrast to physical signs and symbols, physical actions and activities need have no referential qualities whatsoever to be intelligible: instead they must be seen to play a part in some overall scheme of events, to fit a pattern of life in order to be intelligible. Thus the relations to be intuited by the understanding agent in actions and activities are, in the main, *means–end* relations: and this whether the action is purely instrumental or whether it instantiates an end.

Not all means–end relations are identical, of course, but the achievement of an end will be the effectual outcome of the employment of appropriate means, and here one espies a *causal* relation between means and end. Such causal relations may well be internal to any one particular activity and have no reference to the larger pattern of life of which the activity is a part. To understand an activity is not simply to perceive the relations of the activity but also the reasons for the behaviour.

To understand why a person is behaving as he is is to intuit both the *motives* of the agent and the *objective standards* and *canons* determining the rule-governed behaviour. Thus the causal relations perceived when an eight-year-old child is washing up the dishes may be identical with those apparent when that same child is playing with the same objects at the same sink. But the motives of the child, and the standards instantiated in the actions and activities, will differ profoundly from when she is playing to when she is working.

A further set of relations to be intuited in any person's actions are *social parameters*. Faced with the problem of trying to make sense of what is being said, for example, or of what is being done when something is said, one is of necessity driven to ask not only, 'Who said it?' but, furthermore, 'In what context was it said?' The significance of the actor rehearsing his lines in the privacy of his own back garden is different from that of the same actor saying the same lines in a dramatic performance in front of a distinguished audience – and different yet again should he employ those same lines in his private life.

Implicit in such examples are both *spatial* and *temporal* relations because without these no physical object, activity or action is either recognizable or intelligible.

Understanding what is being done is different from understanding how something is done, however. The difference lies herein – that to understand how to perform an action entails the intuition of the principle or principles in accordance with which the action.is performed. Furthermore it is in the grasping of such principles that there lies the difference between understanding how to do something and simply being able to do it. One may do something simply by following instructions successfully: it is not until 'the penny drops' or 'the light dawns' and one perceives the principle(s) inherent in the act that one can be said to understand how this is done.

Such discernment of *principles of action* is not only necessary in understanding how to do something: it is also central to understanding the mechanical functioning of artifacts. To understand how a machine works is not just to trace causal and sequential chains but to do so in the light of their interplay and interdependence the one upon the other, and all upon the end to which each part contributes. It is to understand why such interplay and interdependence of parts must be of one order and none other – and that can only be done if principles are grasped.

The successful functioning of mechanical artifacts is not simply dependent upon the application of principles of action but also upon the employment of appropriate materials, fluids and gases. Their efficient employment lies not simply in the recognition of their properties but in the discernment of the relations of their properties, their potential interaction with each other and the predictive outcome of such interaction. It is the chemical and physical nature of objects which must be discerned. And this is not a matter of tracing detail but of perceiving *theoretical principles* in accordance with which the details make sense.

Implicit in many of the examples chosen so far to illustrate different kinds of relations have been references to mental phenomena. Whether such phenomena are classed as cognitive or affective it is the case that those relations which characterize them are predominantly logical.

Within facts, beliefs, arguments, hypotheses, fears, hopes, dreams, worries and fascinations are to be traced relations of *identity*, *equality* and *entailment*, of *deduction*, *induction* and *inference*, and of *implication* and *correlation*. Without the discernment of such relations (whether or not one can articulate the precise nature of each) thoughts are unintelligible and emotions irrational. Neither the coherent necessity of a valid argument, for example, nor the correspondence of factual statements to what the case is, is intelligible without the intuition of such relations. And in many cases, e.g. dreams and mysteries, it is the very inability to discern explicitly those relations which are so clearly intuited as implicit and necessary which constitutes the difficulty of understanding the phenomena.

In addition to such logical relations in the life of every person there are those of *ontological dependence*. Such relations are those whereby the continued existence of any particular being, or group of beings, is necessarily determined. Examples of such have already been given in chapter 2 where, in explicating the notion of 'person', reference was made to both symbiotic and social relations. And one form of the latter was discussed at some length in section 1 of this chapter in contending that consciousness by way of conceptualization involved the necessity of the individual person standing under the discipline of public schemes of conceptualization.

Such relations of ontological dependence are neither simply physical nor simply intellectual: indeed, in so far as a person is an harmony of many dimensions so the range of relations of ontological dependence is as great as the number of such dimensions. And it will be argued later (in chapter 5) that within the spiritual dimension of life such relations are of prime significance.

The kind of persons we are is constituted by the relations of ontological dependence which constitute the 'grid' or 'pattern' of personhood and personality. But as a person is capable of being autonomous rather than wholly heteronomous with regard to the kind of person he wishes to be, so this implies choice of the particular ontological relations he establishes. Such choice implies the presence of values.

Now whilst some things are valuable as means to ends, others are held to be intrinsically valuable – and this is not simply a contingent matter but a necessary fact because unless there are certain intrinsically valuable 'objects' there arise problems of an infinite regress in any means–end series of values. This being so, it is obvious that in endeavouring to understand a person it is important to identify that which is of supreme intrinsic worth to that person.

Such a 'supreme worth' will necessarily be of intrinsic value to the person who adheres to it. But it may not be the only thing which he regards as intrinsically valuable. There may be other things in life which are such but which are nevertheless not regarded as of supreme worth by an individual agent. Thus the man who regards 'W' as of supreme worth may also hold 'X', 'Y' and 'Z' to be intrinsically valuable also, but of less worth to him – even though they be part of his life.

Given that a person is living a united and harmonious life, then those matters which he regards as intrinsically valuable must be reconciled in some way – they must be connected or related. Such a relation will necessarily be one in terms of values held by the agent and in terms of his own evaluation of his situation in the light of these values. Accordingly, in understanding a person, it is not simply a matter of perceiving relations of ontological dependence but also a matter of tracing those values whereby the subject determines his own agency. Thus relations between values – *value gradations* – need to be discerned.

Such advertence to just some of the relations inherent in objects which are discerned by the understanding mind gives insight into both the complexity and potential richness of human understanding. As an intellectual phenomenon 'understanding' is complex to the point of appearing paradoxical: and cognizance of the variety of relations which may be discerned by the understanding mind suggests that one feature of this complexity is the sheer variety of possible insights.

Such complexity and potential richness of human understanding is traditionally referred to in terms of its 'breadth and depth'. In attempting to explicate this feature of understanding in the next section it must be borne in mind that one of the features of understanding which must be accounted for is that of the unity of such complexity. Talk about 'breadth' of understanding often implies successful intuition in more than one logically distinct kind of understanding. Yet, as has been argued already, it is a regular feature of understanding that it unifies distinct and diverse stimuli and perceptions in theoretical wholes.

Understanding always tends towards theoretical entities: it always harmonizes and welds together in new wholes that which is apparently diverse, including distinct relations. Accordingly any attempt to analyse the breadth and depth of understanding must account for this unity of diversity, and this diversity in unity.

4 Breadth and depth of understanding

Our discussion of the unified richness and complexity of a person's understanding may be undertaken by considering the matter in three ways. In the first place we may consider what might be meant by 'a fully developed understanding'. This will bring us necessarily head on to an analysis of 'breadth and depth of understanding'. Second – and consequent upon this analysis – we may discuss what might be termed 'weak' or 'early' understanding. Finally we may attempt to explicate formal differences between logically distinct kinds of understanding.

(i) *Potential for rational insight* By a 'fully developed understanding' is not meant a total and complete understanding of all objects which a person may comprehend. Rather it implies potential. As an interactive state of creative intuition 'understanding' may be said to be fully developed when that interaction, which is creative intuition, is free to continue in a cumulative manner. 'Interaction' implies continuous development and not eschatological staticity: so a 'fully developed understanding' is necessarily one which is capable of further efficient accumulation of insight.

The insights discerned in this state of creative intuition must

84

be logically cogent and true – otherwise there arises misunder-standing. Thus implicit in the notion of a 'fully developed understanding' is the idea that any person who may be credited with such is one who knows and employs criteria of logical cogency and truth. Furthermore, he must be aware of those methods and procedures which instantiate such criteria for both the establishment of the rationality of the insights and the intuition of further insights. 'Fully developed under-standing' is a creative potential circumscribed by rational requirements.

The rationality of distinct endeavours is not identical, how-ever. It could never be insisted that there is no rational differ-ence between decarbonizing an engine and studying an histor-ical period, between making a cake and reading a novel. A rational endeavour is rational in terms of the particular pat-tern of interaction. Criteria of logical cogency and truth are therefore as particular as the particularity of each rational endeavour.

A 'fully developed understanding' is the potential for the creative intuition of relations in a diversity of rational endeavours and objects: 'understanding' is not monolithic but a 'family of kinds of understanding'. Understanding how to maintain a car in good condition is other than understanding how to do history – and likewise how to bake cakes and read novels. And it is because of this that there is talk of 'breadth' of understanding: there is an extensiveness of understanding which has to do with the different kinds of understanding of which a person is capable.

Such breadth of understanding is not fragmentary insight, however, but, as all understanding is unifying insight, so breadth of understanding has to do both with the intuition of 'internal' relations within particular endeavours and objects and also insight in the 'external' relations between diverse phenomena.[12]

(ii) *Unity of insight*   Such unifying breadth of understanding may be illustrated by reference to that most popular of 'objects to be understood', the motor car. It is a truism that, mechani-cally speaking, the vehicle may be understood as a combina-tion of dissimilar and separate systems – e.g. the braking, steering, fuelling, exhausting, power producing, power transmitting systems, etc. Each of these systems may be viewed as complete in itself and the relations 'internal' to each system may be intuited. But it is the relations between the systems, which are 'external' to each system, which must also be perceived if the car as a whole is to be understood mechanically. General car maintenance requires breadth of mechanical understanding.

Such breadth of *mechanical* understanding is not the complete story of breadth of understanding of the motor car. The vehicle may also be comprehended in, say, aesthetic, economic, sociological, historical and religious ways. Each of the individual systems in a motor car, as well as the car as a whole, may be understood mechanically and in these other ways. Thus 'breadth of understanding' of the motor car implies the intuition of (i) internal relations, (ii) external relations, and (iii) relations of the numerous ways in which a single object may be understood.

'Breadth of understanding' is a necessary feature of the interactive and unifying nature of all understanding. There is, on the one hand, the 'givenness' of the motor car – one cannot do just anything one wishes with steel, oil, water and rubber – and, on the other hand, there are the numerous forms of appreciation of such relations which man employs. 'Breadth of understanding' implies extensiveness of both and the unity of insight consequent upon the creative interaction of both.

'Breadth of understanding' has to do with the unity of diverse insight: and a fully developed understanding is one whose potential for creative intuition is such that those relations which are constitutive of the unity of life may be correctly perceived. But as well as such qualities a fully developed understanding also manifests qualities of 'depth': and such depth of understanding has to do with clarity of insight on the one hand and the level of insight on the other hand. It is a matter of seeing correct relations clearly and of grasping their nature firmly.

(iii) *Clarity of insight*   Shallow understanding is not ignorance but puzzlement. It is not total absence of insight but blurred, confused perception. One says, 'I think I understand, but I'm not sure': and that is quite different from saying, 'I do not understand.' In Whitehead's words, understanding 'is the self-evidence of pattern, so far as it has been discriminated'[13] and in so far as the self-evident pattern is obviously evident to the observer so his understanding of the matter has depth: and in so far as such self-evidence is not obvious to the observer so his understanding is shallow.

Clarity of insight is the penetrative power of the mind to theorize: and the value of any theory lies in its simplicity and universality. To discern lucidly is to grasp the essential oneness of anything in terms of its parts and at the same time to perceive the necessary relationships of parts whereby universals are constituted and maintained. The degree to which this analytic/synthetic movement can be harnessed and employed is the measure of the depth of a person's understanding. And, incidentally, one thus begins to see that breadth and depth of understanding are not 'separate' aspects of insight but are in fact intimately related.

Depth of understanding, however, is always a matter of clarity of insight: but not all insights are 'direct'. In Lonergan's terms, some are 'inverse'. Objects are presented by the senses or by the imagination and one endeavours to make sense of them. But some objects lack logical coherence: and depth of understanding manifests itself in perceiving that what is self-evident in them is this very lack of pattern.[14]

> While direct insight grasps the point, or sees the solution, or comes to know the reason, inverse insight apprehends that in some fashion the point is that there is no point, or that the solution is to deny the solution, or that the reason is that the rationality of the real admits distinctions and qualifications.

Such subtle and critical discernment is missing in shallow understanding which often wishes to insist on the validity of 'direct' insight alone.

(iv) *Levels of insight* Besides 'clarity of insight' depth of understanding also implies 'level of insight'. There are different levels of insight and there can be clarity of insight at each level. Now the causes of this need not concern us here: what matters is the explication of the levels of insight at which relations may be intuited.

That level of insight to which attention may be drawn first may be termed the *concrete* level – that is, the 'sense perceptible' level of intuition. In the case of animals and young children it seems to be the case that only those things can be understood of which the necessary relations can in some way be illustrated physically. So a child may 'hear' relations between musical notes and express that relation by singing the notes long before he can say anything about the intervals. Again, a child may be able to show one the way to his home and yet not be able to direct one there even though he be a 'real chatterbox'.

This concrete level of insight remains with us throughout life. Faced with a piece of machinery which will not work, or a complex dress pattern to be made up, we comment, 'It's no good: I'll have to lay it out on the floor.' We are then operating at the concrete level of insight: of only being able to intuit relations between objects when those objects are sensibly proximate to each other.

The concrete level of insight is obviously highly particular and contingent in scope: the relations intuited lack any universal quality and therefore the discernment does not aid unifying breadth of understanding. It is only at the second level of insight that relations of a universal nature are intuited. This level may be termed the *conceptual* level of insight because the relations are both perceived and grasped through the employment of concepts, and are expressed in conceptual symbols.

At this conceptual level of insight the relations are discerned as not simply found in particular, individual phenomena but throughout man's interactive experience of all similar phenomena. Thus, to return to examples of machinery and dress patterns – at the concrete level of insight there will be intuited those relations pertaining to just the one example laid out on the floor in front of us. Those same relations may be intuited at a conceptual level also: that is, the relations will be perceived as pertinent to a whole class of objects and practices.

It is this conceptual level of insight which is at work, therefore, in theoretical studies and in discerning the principles of action. 'Being able to do something', for example, may simply involve insight at the concrete level: 'grasping the principles of the activity' necessitates intuition at the conceptual level.

The conceptual level of insight differs from the concrete level in terms of 'abstraction': the relations are intuited as being involved in more than just one set of circumstances, or one object, and are to this extent less object-bound. Nevertheless, at the conceptual level of insight relations are still perceived as necessarily rooted in, and manifested by, overt physical phenomena.

The abstractive process may continue and a third level of insight is achieved when the nature of the relations is itself intuited. Thus spatial, temporal and causal relations may all be perceived at concrete and conceptual levels of insight: but each kind of relation may itself be understood as of a particular nature. What is perceived here is in fact the form of the relation: so this level of insight may be termed the *formal* level.

The fourth and final level of insight is the *metaphysical*. Whilst the particularity of the concrete level of insight requires little emphasis, what does require underlining is the fact that both conceptual and formal levels of insight are often particularized by both the class of objects understood and by the way of appreciation employed in understanding those objects. It is quite common, for example, for one person to achieve conceptual and formal levels of insight in, say, art and aesthetics and not in, say, biology or social history. There is thus limited breadth and depth of understanding.

If there is to be extensive depth and breadth of understanding of man's position and status then there must be insight into the interrelatedness of life in its wholeness and totality: and such breadth of understanding implies a depth which is of high generality and universality. Obviously such depth implies a formal level of insight: and yet it is the kind of insight which is deeper than the formal level in any one way of understanding. At the metaphysical level of insight relations of high abstraction are perceived as constitutive of the universality and unity of the multifarious diversity of personal life.

(v) *The necessary interrelatedness of breadth and depth of understanding*   With these four levels of insight in mind – the concrete, conceptual, formal and metaphysical – it may now be seen that breadth and depth of understanding are more closely logically interrelated than their 'quantitative' and 'qualitative' tones suggest. The promotion of breadth of understanding necessarily implies the intuition of relations at conceptual, formal and metaphysical levels of insight: and the clarity of discernment at different levels of insight requires both a variety of objects to be understood together with a diversity of ways of appreciation.

The interrelationship of breadth and depth of understanding is such that we must avoid 'the bewitchment of language' which prompts us to believe that there can be breadth of understanding without depth, and vice versa. It must be contended that such is their logical interdependence that there can be no breadth of understanding without depth, and no depth of understanding without breadth. They are but two sides of the same coin.

The function of intellectual understanding is the creative intuition of correct relations, and its intellectual goal is that of unifying insight, and this being so it follows that a fully developed understanding is not one which operates simply at a metaphysical level of insight. To understand his position and status man, as a physical being, needs to be able to discern relations at concrete and conceptual levels also. In fact a fully developed understanding is one in which there is a marked felicity for operating at all levels of insight as and when this is appropriate.

It is very often the case that unified insight into a particular situation necessitates fluidity of movement between levels of insight and not simply discernment at one particular level. All too often metaphysical speculation of a universalizing nature is shown to be bankrupt because it has ignored insight at concrete and conceptual levels: and many endeavours embracing discernments at concrete and conceptual levels of insight have been dangerous because they have ignored 'wider implications' to be perceived at formal and metaphysical levels of insight.

To understand fully is to intuit relations both of a universal and of a particular nature, and the depth of understanding which is insight into universal unity of diverse phenomena is the breadth of understanding which discerns the necessary interaction of separable particulars. Indeed, to the extent that relations are intuited at formal and metaphysical levels so insight into the nature of particulars is both enriched and clarified. Conversely, any deep understanding of particulars is contributory to the elimination of erroneous insights on a universal scale. Thus a full understanding of particulars necessarily implies a breadth of understanding on a universal scale: whilst a unified understanding of separable particulars on a universal scale necessarily implies insight into the 'internal' relations of particulars. Such dialectical movement is logically impossible without discernment at different levels of insight. It therefore follows that whilst 'breadth' and 'depth' of understanding may be separable for purposes of academic advertence, nevertheless 'breadth' without 'depth', and 'depth' without 'breadth' of understanding is in essence a logical impossibility.

(vi) *Early understanding as 'puzzlement'* In contrast to fully developed understanding is 'early' or 'shallow' understanding: and attention was drawn earlier to the fact that shallow understanding is not ignorance, or complete and total lack of understanding, but puzzlement.

Puzzlement is always the intuition of the necessity of relations but a vague and imprecise intuition such that one feels, rather than perceives, that there is some way forward towards intellectual comprehension yet that way eludes one's discernment. Such puzzlement, evident in both children and adults at times, is lack of freedom to creatively intuit relations correctly and clearly. It is a failure to accumulate insights – and this may occur at any of the four levels of insight identified above. (Indeed, early philosophical understanding comprises puzzlement at the formal level of insight.)

Now it is a common adage that 'if one doesn't ask the right question, one doesn't receive the right answer' and inherent in a great deal of puzzlement is a failure of insight of a very peculiar kind – *viz*. that of identification of the problem. It is a psychological fact – and not a logical truth – that human understanding is often 'triggered off' when persons are faced with faults, breakdowns, diseases, questions, failures and problems of one kind or another. It is a logical fact – and not a psychological truth – that the accumulation of insights is necessarily dependent upon the identification of the problem.

Unless an object to be understood is correctly identified, and its constituent parts laid out, it is impossible for the pattern of necessary relations which unite the parts in the whole to be discerned. That puzzlement which accompanies the early stages of any understanding is partially a failure to recognize clearly the very object which is to be understood, and often this is a matter of the inadequacy of the description under which the object is to be comprehended.

(vii) *The novice status of early understanding* Many of the objects to be understood, together with the conceptual schemes employed to describe them, are often only of significance to us in so far as they further, or thwart, our endeavours. Thus an adequate description of something (say, a library, vacuum flask, refrigerator) is often pertinent and accurate as much in 'functional' terms as in 'physical' terms. To this extent Wittgenstein was right to emphasize that a 'language-game' is a 'form of life'. The depth of our understanding is intimately related to the measure of our participation and involvement in human endeavours: and early understanding is novice status in a walk of life.

All forms of life involve not merely the recognition of objects to be understood but also the appreciation of what is significant and pertinent, and the evaluation of what is right and proper. Some methods are more profitable than others, some processes more relevant than others, and some procedures happier than others. Moreover there are procedures for applying canons of profitability, relevance and happiness. These also must be learned by the novice because they constitute the rationale of the way of life: and to the extent that he has not mastered these procedures and made them his own so the agent's understanding will necessarily be limited and shallow because, as was argued earlier, the criterion of success of the interaction which is understanding is the rationality of the insight.

To the extent to which intuition of relations is circumscribed by considerations of logical cogency and truth so it is developed. And in so far as understanding anything is a creative act on the part of each individual agent so his intuition of unifying relations and his grasp of what constitutes the relevance, significance, pertinence and truth of insights goes hand in hand. In this sense fully developed understanding is 'autonomous' but early understanding is 'heteronomous' because the agent is not in a position to know whether or not his intuitions are veridical.

(viii) *The fragmentary nature of early understanding* If the heteronomy of the agent is a feature of early understanding – both in terms of the statement of the problem and in the application of methods of procedure – then another feature of shallow understanding is its isolated, piecemeal nature. Early understanding often exhibits a marked absence of any breadth being unrelated to other facts and practices that the agent already knows and comprehends. This is only to be expected because, as has been argued, breadth of understanding goes hand in hand with depth of understanding, and as much early understanding takes place at a low level of insight so it is impossible for there to be breadth of understanding.

Those relations which subsist between separate physical objects and ways of appreciation are viewed at conceptual, formal and metaphysical levels of insight rather than at the concrete level: and it is not until understanding has been deepened to these levels that breadth of understanding can be promoted apace. Indeed, so much early understanding takes place at the concrete level of insight that it is not surprising that it is piecemeal.

As a general rule it may be mooted that any early particular kind of understanding always takes place at a level of insight lower than that at which that fully developed kind of understanding normally operates. Moreover, as in fully developed understanding the mind slips happily from one level of insight to another, so in early understanding perception across the levels of insight is absent.

It may be argued therefore that early, or shallow, understanding is a form of puzzlement, a novice status characterized by the intuition of the necessity of relations coupled with failure to accumulate insights; the partial failure to firmly apprehend the object to be understood; the incomplete grasp of the rationale of the form of life; the fragmentary nature of insight; insight at a lower level than that at which a fully developed understanding normally operates; and, an inability to comprehend relations at different levels of insight.

(ix) *Formal differences between kinds of understanding* Implicit in the foregoing remarks is the belief that the understanding of any particular object is in fact a unified amalgam of different ways of understanding that object. A chair, for example, may be understood functionally, chemically, historically and religiously and in many other ways: and a total understanding of the chair is a unity of these different kinds of comprehension. It may be profitable, therefore, to indicate briefly the formal differences between such kinds of understanding.

As an intellectual phenomenon any kind of understanding is goal-oriented. It is concerned with achieving the particular end of unifying insight by means of the intuition of necessary relations. This being so it may be argued that what characterizes a particular kind of understanding is, in the first place, the particular kinds of relations which are to be intuited.

This intuition of particular kinds of relations is a necessary product of man's interaction with his environment and therefore the particularity of the relations intuited is as much dependent upon the appreciative powers of man employed in his intellectual strivings as upon the nature of the cosmos which is 'given'. It has already been argued (in section 1) that any understanding of any kind involves that form of consciousness which is the apprehension of objects by way of accurate description, and this has been shown to involve consciousness by way of conceptualization. It therefore follows that the intuition of particular kinds of relations is associated with the categories and concepts employed in apprehending objects.

The understanding of an object does not entail the intuition of just any relations, it has been argued, but those which are correct: any form of understanding is one in which due regard is given to rationality – to logical cogency and truth. The 'truth procedures' necessary to any kind of understanding will there-fore constitute a further formal characteristic of a kind of understanding.

Those procedures whereby truth criteria are applied must not be confused with other procedures within an activity whereby that activity is pushed forward. The steps one takes in doing a piece of woodwork, for example, are sometimes other than the application of canons of efficiency, efficacy and beauty. But such 'practical' procedures are no less important than those of 'evaluation' in terms of the promotion of insights. This being so, a particular kind of understanding will be characterized by those procedures which assist in furthering the perception of necessary relations.

Finally it may be observed that whilst there is no necessary connection between the possession of insight and its public demonstration – a matter which will be returned to in the next section – it is a fact that certain particular patterns of observ-able behaviour are associated with particular kinds of under-standing. The equation is as much at home in expressing mathematical insight as the essay is in demonstrating historical insight.

A particular kind of understanding is therefore to be charac-terized formally as a form of unifying insight concerned with the intuition of specific kinds of necessary relations; employ-ing particular conceptual schemes to apprehend objects; employing distinct criteria of logical cogency and truth; pro-moted by the taking of particular procedural steps; and, often demonstrated in particular ways.

We thus observe that the unity of a person's understanding of objects is both highly complex in terms of its potential variety of insights and rich in terms of its potential depth and breadth. And our thesis is that such complexity and richness is only intelligible in terms of subjective-objective, private-public, individual-social interactions. The relation between the private and public side of understanding is seen to be totally necessary and not merely accidental: but this is not to argue that it is a simple and obvious relation. This point may be finally argued by giving some consideration both to what might be meant by 'the understanding' and to 'the public demonstration of insight'.

5 The understanding and the public demonstration of insight

(i) *The innate powers of the mind*   In attempting to understand understanding there arise questions of a necessary kind regarding those features and powers of the mind involved in a subject's interaction with the cosmos. It has long been a tradition to speak of 'the understanding' as part of the mind and, although such talk smacks of faculty psychology, it is nevertheless true that the identification of the mental powers necessarily involved in a person's understanding objects is of importance – and that, not simply from a logical, philosophical point of view, but also from a practical, educational standpoint.

One of the difficulties of this task is that of separating out logically necessary mental powers from contingent social and psychological factors. It is common experience, for example, that one often moves from puzzlement to intellectual comprehension at times when one is neither tired, worried nor jaundiced. But to say that a good night's sleep, or a fortnight's holiday, assists understanding is to draw attention to aids to understanding rather than to what is logically necessary. In a similar way, one's social boundaries, especially when one is young, may either stimulate intellectual comprehension or stultify it. And the cultural milieu in which one lives will provide categories, concepts and intellectual goals such as to delimit one's outlook on life.

Such aids and limitations are not those powers of the mind logically necessary to the understanding of objects. That they may facilitate, or hamper, understanding cannot be denied: but that which is logically necessary to provocation of insight is the innate powers of the mind which constitute the understanding, which each person brings to bear upon his environment.

(ii) *Sense perception*   In the opening paragraph proper of his book *Human Understanding*, Toulmin insists that[15]

> human understanding has developed historically in two complementary ways . . . Looking 'outside ourselves'

and mastering the problems posed by the world we live in, we have extended our understanding; looking 'inwards' and considering how it is that we master those problems, we have deepened it.

And in these terms it may be argued that those powers of the mind which constitute the understanding are those of 'looking' and 'mastering'. Thus one of the powers is sense perception.

Our senses are our windows on the world. Without our senses there would be no interaction of any kind whatsoever between individual persons and their environment. Without sense percepts there would be no receipt of causal stimuli, no presentation of objects, no adequate description and apprehension of things. The concrete level of insight would be impossible and, in so far as this is often crucial in our understanding of anything, so there would be no understanding whatsoever.

The idea of some *res cogitans* contemplating its own deliberations devoid of sense percepts is illogical in personal terms because so many of such personal deliberations implicitly assume an experience of sensible objects, and a retention of sense percepts, which cannot be reduced to any theoretical conceptual description. Thus the commonplace muddiness of mud, wetness of water and abrasive hardness of concrete are matters of sense perception: they are percepts which cannot be wholly and significantly conveyed in theoretical concepts. Sense perception is a constitutive element of a person's understanding.

(iii) *Conceptualization* Encountering objects and acquiring sense percepts is one thing: but for the interactive state of creative intuition to arise there must be recognition of things for what they are. In order to understand things, situations, places and people as such one needs to identify them as such and not just to encounter them.

This point has already been argued at length in section 1: we may therefore simply reiterate that there can be no comprehension of objects unless the descriptions of the objects are themselves clear and accurate. There can be no consciousness of the real as the real without concept possession: consciousness by way of conceptualization is an inherent feature of a person's understanding of anything. The innate power of conceptualization is necessary to understanding.

(iv) *Imagination*   By means of sense perception and conceptualization all kinds of knowledge and information is acquired and mastered. But understanding an object is other than knowing it. The essence of understanding is intellectual perception – the penetrative power of the mind to theorize in an analytic/synthetic manner. And for such insight the imagination is required.

One is almost fearful of saying anything about imagination these days when the term is bandied about so much. But there are three different 'kinds' of imagination which are constitutive powers of the understanding. And, first, is the ability to image. Descartes seems to have this meaning in mind when he wrote,[16]

> when I imagine a triangle I not only conceive it as a figure composed of three lines, but moreover consider these three lines as being present by the power and internal application of my mind, and that is properly what I call imagining.

Such a power is obviously highly necessary to the understanding for it enables the mind to present to itself images for contemplation – and such may be images of objects which were once present but are now absent; images (such as Descartes' triangle) which facilitate the grasp of conceptual descriptions; and images of possible arrangements and potential patterns. Moreover, by being able to image the mind is able all the more easily to slip from the concrete level of insight to those other levels and thus 'imagination' in this sense is necessary not simply to the contemplation of objects but to the deepening perception of relations.

A second sense of imagination is that of 'supposition' or 'hypothesization' – an 'if . . . then' projection of ideas and possibilities. This is necessary for both breadth and depth of understanding because without it perception of the unity of diverse insights would never begin, the discernment of possible steps to be taken in an endeavour would be impossible, and the floating of novel patterns and models of intellectual advancement would cease. Depth of understanding always implies insight-which-is-foresight: one sees this in the planning of itineraries, the framing of constitutions, the repairing of pieces of machinery and the tracing of consequences of action. Such foresight would be impossible without supposition.

The third meaning of imagination is 'fantasy'. Thus stories, plays, films, music may all be truly fantastic and full of phantoms. And as long as there is no confusion of the real and the fantastic, such imaginative thinking is central to understanding anything by way of contrasting the real with the fantastic, and so making the real more vivid, and by way of highlighting features in real life which are often ignored or just taken for granted.

In these three senses of 'imagination' the imagination is logically necessary to deepening and broadening a person's understanding of objects. It is by way of the imagination that analyses and syntheses are first mooted, novel ideas and patterns first embraced, and implicit relations explicitly entertained. But the very fantasizing element of the imagination is such that, by itself, it is liable to lead to as much misunderstanding as understanding of objects and accordingly there must be another power of the mind capable of discerning the necessary correctness of relations intuited.

(v) *Ratiocinative reflection*   This fourth power of the mind is ratiocinative reflection. At the risk of being repetitive, it must be emphasized that understanding anything is the intuition of correct and necessary relations in depth and breadth. For this ratiocinative reflection is necessary.

It is by means of reflection that criteria of truth, significance, relevance and pertinence are applied so that the true is apprehended as the true, the significant as the significant, the relevant as the relevant and the pertinent as the pertinent. It is by reflection that paradoxes are resolved or rejected and antinomies evaporated or cast out. It is by reflection that we marshal and weigh evidence, drag up instances and counterinstances from the memory, recognize pertinent principles and evaluate and judge locutions.

99

Reflection is not simply the gateway to the intuition of correct relations, however: it is also the path to extending and deepening our insight. By the making of inferences, deductions and inductions we extend our understanding of this world: and by casting new moulds of thought – by replacing old concepts and paradigms in innovatory fashion – we reconsider old problems afresh. Moreover, the happy employment of all levels of insight, and the dialectical transition from concrete and conceptual levels of insight to formal and metaphysical levels is only possible by dint of reflection. This is one of the paradoxes of understanding (resolved only in terms of 'interaction') that by looking 'inwards' (to use Toulmin's word) our understanding of the 'outer' word is enhanced. Such enhancement is impossible without reflection.

Sense perception, conceptualization, imagination and reflection are innate powers of the mind necessarily involved in a person's understanding of objects. But as a quartet of mental powers they are not sufficient to characterize the understanding: all four may equally well be found in other mental phenomena. Though they are necessary they require one 'catalyst', as it were, to combine and weld them into the understanding.

(vi) *Creative intuition*   That innate power of the mind which is unique in understanding is the power of creative intuition. Whilst the four mental powers indicated above are necessarily involved in the understanding, that which gives them direction, and which provides them with the 'telos' which is distinctive of the understanding, is that power of the mind to employ these powers in a creative manner and to perceive intellectually.

The passivity of the understanding whereby it receives causal stimuli, communal categories and psychological promptings can never be denied: but its hallmark is its creative activity. The understanding does not just draw further inferences in addition to those already drawn; neither does it manufacture yet another effect to be added to those already caused; and neither does it deduce yet another statement from the myriad of statements stated. Instead it rises above all symbolic expressions, all chains of justification, all definitions of terms and descriptions of objects to create a new whole, an insight.

It is because of this creative power of the mind on the part of each individual person that it is a logical truth – and not simply an empirical fact – that the individual person can only come to understand something for himself. Moreover, it is because insight is created 'as a new one' that those intuitions often seem to come in a flash, as a revelation, and with Archimedes one cries 'Eureka!'

The understanding is always creative and it is for this reason that comprehension is so often accompanied by delight (because who does not enjoy creating something new of and for themselves ?): but it is also often accompanied by feelings of relief and surprise at one's own previous blindness. And these latter feelings are only to be expected once it is realized that what is created is nothing less than intuition of necessary and correct relations. 'It is all so obvious' once the light has dawned and the relation has been intuited – because it is all so necessary. Anyone can propose contingent and possible relations by the dozen: only the person who understands perceives the necessary and correct relations.

We may therefore assert that 'the understanding' is that intellectual amalgam of sense perception, conceptualization, imagination and reflection blended and compounded with the power of creative intuition. And we may argue that these are innate powers which the human mind brings to bear in any personal interaction with the given cosmos. But even though such powers are both innate and logically necessary to understanding objects this is no guarantee that there will be intuition of correct and necessary relations on the part of any individual agent. Becoming an understanding person has much to do with associating with others who either possess intellectual insights already or who are struggling to do so. And such social interaction presupposes the feasibility of the public demonstration of insight.

(vii) *Logical difficulties of the demonstration of insight* The belief that private intellectual comprehension can be publicly manifested is so strong that many have come to explicate the very meaning of 'understanding' in terms of overt behaviour. The crucial point here, however, is the distinction between evidence of possession of insight and criteria of understanding. The fact is that public performances and behaviour need not be evidence of understanding whereas such alone can be the only observables to which one may apply criteria of understanding.

The etymology of the word 'evidence' (Latin *e-videre*) indicates that that which is evidential is that which is visible, obvious and conspicuous. Now whilst a person's actions and performances may be observable they cannot always be taken as evidence of his understanding or of his failure to understand. An agent may regularly perform an action correctly without necessarily understanding how it should be done properly. It is a matter of chance or accident. In a similar way a response to an order, command, prescription or request may well be appropriate but is in fact a guess on the part of the agent. The giving of explanations and interpretations is no sure guide for these may be learned by rote and voiced by way of reaction to particular stimuli. Moreover, in all human behaviour there is the ubiquitous possibility of both deception of others and of self-deception.

The problem is that patterns of behaviour are no sure guide to a person's understanding: yet public behaviour alone is the locus for the application of criteria of understanding.

(viii) *Criteria of understanding*   By a criterion is meant 'a standard of judging': and by 'criteria of understanding' can be meant either 'standards of judging whether or not a person does understand', or, 'standards of judging whether or not an insight is correct'. The latter criteria are rooted in and stem from ongoing public traditions and will be as various as these traditions. The former are of a pragmatic nature and relate to both the particularity of the relations to be discerned and to the consistency of the agent's behaviour.

For a person's claim to understand a particular object to be upheld, that same person must demonstrate in his behaviour that he discerns the necessary relations appertaining to the logic of the object. The tests which instantiate such a criterion will be as diverse as the discernible relations. Thus a person may demonstrate his understanding of an argument by drawing inferences from it; an action, by telling or showing how it might be done; and a work of art by offering an interpretation. Such tests instantiate the criterion without being the criterion itself.

The problem is, however, that overt behaviour does not necessarily evidence possession of insight: therefore, it must surely be the case that, for a person's claim to understand an object to be upheld, that same person must *regularly and consistently* demonstrate in his behaviour that he discerns the necessary relations appertaining to the logic of the object.

Herein lies the pragmatic element inasmuch as a person will be allowed his claim to understand an object just as long as his behaviour appears to demonstrate the presence and correctness of insight. The number of tests an agent would have to do successfully is not something that can be determined with any exactness but there needs to be a sufficient number to permit diversity of testing procedures in order to obviate the dangers of (self-) deception.

(ix) *Symbolic expressions of insight* Public expressions of understanding are as numerous as the classes of objects to be understood. The spoken and written word have no monopoly here. Non-verbal art forms of dance, ritual, architecture, music and sculpture may all on occasions be expressions of insight: and in action, reaction, pleasurable activity and work a person may manifest understanding.

Some of these expressions may be fairly clear and direct demonstrations of an agent's understanding but more often they will veil as much as they reveal. And this is a matter of both the logical relationship between insight and behaviour and the ability of the agent to express himself clearly and unambiguously. For it must never be forgotten that it can never be asserted unequivocally that if a person cannot demonstrate his understanding of an object in some publicly observable way then he does not understand that object.

When a locution, action, activity or artifact is expressive of insight it is to that extent symbolic. There can be no 'literal' embodiment of intellectual intuitions in sounds, artifacts and actions because the nature of each is entirely different. Intellectual insight is other than physical objects: so when physical phenomena are employed to express, convey or provoke intellectual discernment they must necessarily function symbolically.

The conclusion is forced upon us that, whilst overt behaviour is not to be identified with the creative intuition of relations, nevertheless when such behaviour is symbolic it is the public manifestation of the functioning of the private understanding. The physical symbol is therefore the means of interaction whereby the powers of each individual person's mind which constitute the understanding unite in public, social harmony and discourse. Without the physical symbol there would be no understanding of anything for that interactive state of creative intuition, which is a constant private-public relation, would never come about.

Chapter 5

Religious understanding

Spirituality is: the power of a man's understanding
over his life.

S. Kierkegaard: Journals, 1851

Introduction

It has been argued in chapters 2 and 3 that religiously educational activities provoke intellectual understanding of the
spirituality of personal life: but our study of intellectual understanding in chapter 4 has led us to observe that such insight is
by no means 'single-track' but a unity of a variety of kinds of
understanding. In this chapter an attempt will be made to
become clear about the precise meaning of 'religious understanding' of objects in contradistinction to what will be called
the 'scholarly understanding' of religion.

An attempt will be made to show that the religious understanding of a man, a social institution or an event, for example,
is other than a scholar's understanding of the religious dimension of personal life in its many manifestations. It will be
argued that both forms of understanding are necessary for
religious education and that depth and breadth of scholarly
understanding of religion is logically dependent upon the
provocation of religious understanding of objects.

1 The nature of religious understanding

(i) *Its practicality*   In the light of the earlier analyses of 'religion' and 'understanding' it follows necessarily that the religious understanding of objects implies the apprehension of
those objects in spiritual terms and the intuition of relations
which are primarily those of ontological dependence and
evaluative gradation.

It must be the case that religiously understood objects are
apprehended in spiritual terms because 'religion' necessarily
implies 'spirituality'. And whilst such a form of comprehension does not necessitate the discernment only of relations of
ontological dependence and evaluation, nevertheless the
nature of the religious dimension of personal life is such that
the intuition of such relations is of prime concern.

This primary concern with such relations is perceived as
necessary once it is appreciated that the religious dimension of
personal life is essentially practical and not theoretical. It has
already been argued that the appropriate response of the individual person in a spiritual interaction is one of faith and not
one of attempted intellectual mastery. Religious knowledge,
for example, is not primarily propositional knowledge but
knowledge-which-is-union[1] and procedural knowledge.
Religious language (in theistic terms) is talking to God and
fellow-man and not talking about God and fellow-man.

To be a subject in communion with the infinite and essential
ultimate reality is necessarily to be active. The infinitizing of
the dependent and vulnerable self by means of self-sacrifice
and pure communion with ultimate spiritual reality is
achieved by means of action, activity and adoption of appropriate attitudes rather than by way of intellectual theorizing
and hypothesizing. It is such practical involvement which is
implicit in popular descriptions of religion as 'a way of life' and
as 'a personal matter'.

Religious understanding is not less intellectual than, say,
scientific, historical or mathematical understanding. It is its
intellectual goal which is different. Historical understanding,
for example, has as its intellectual goal the broadening and
deepening of historical insight. It is thoroughly academic. Any

'practical' inferences drawn from its insights regarding the present are of no concern to the historian as an historian. Indeed, many would question the possibility of drawing such practical inferences.

Religious understanding is, in contrast, utterly practical and contemporary. Its *raison d'être* is not its own furtherance as an academic pursuit but the intensification of the union of the self with ultimate spiritual reality. It is the discernment of those steps which must be taken within the spriutal dimension of life by the man of faith: its intellectual goal is the intuition of those relations which are inherent in the logic of the life of religious faith.

(ii) *Relations of ontological dependence*   Implicit in the logic of the life of religious faith are relations of ontological dependence. Our analysis of the concept of 'person' has shown that personal life is impossible without such relations. Some of these are physical, others mental and social. Religious understanding discerns such relations in the spiritual dimension of personal life.

Personal life requires a 'grid' of relations of ontological dependence: and because the religious life is that of the spiritual dimension of personal life so the discernment of spiritual relations of ontological dependence is of prime concern in religious understanding. The abundant life for the religious man is the spiritual life and so he must root himself in the spiritual ultimacy of the cosmos.

(iii) *Value relations*   This discernment of spiritual relations of ontological dependence necessarily implies the perception of relations of comparative value also. Outside the spiritual dimension of life such a necessary relation between what is and what ought to be would not hold: but an outstanding feature of the religious dimension of life is that this distinction between 'is' and 'ought' is transcended and that which ultimately 'is' is held to be of greatest value.

This distinction between the real and the good is evaporated in the religious life in practical terms because the establishment of relations of ontological dependence is pursued by way of adverting to values and qualities of life and by way of their instantiation in action. Thus, in the Christian religion, the establishment of the ontological relations between God and man is the pursuit of loving action. To be ontologically related to God is to love: and to be loving is to be with God.

Religious understanding is peculiar and particular inasmuch as ontological relations are intuited in terms of values, and relations of comparative value are discerned in ontological terms. To enter into a spiritual relationship is to abide by values: and it is the quality of life which is the measure of spiritual ontology. Thus a religious understanding of, say, the legends of Elijah is not the discernment of socio-political relations in Israel and Tyre in the ninth century BC but the perception of the significance of 'purity' in the spiritual life: and the religious understanding of the resurrection of Jesus is not the discernment of chronological factors but the intuition of the might of personal love to overcome the apparently supreme limitation of death.

(iv) *The discernment of ontic values*   The primary intuition of any kind of religious understanding is the discernment of ontic values. Examples of such from the Christian religion are love, patience, mercy, pity, charity, sympathy, self-sacrifice, self-abasement, reverence, chastity and humility. These are *ontic* values because they are the very structure of the spiritual subject: they are the actual constituents of a person's spiritual nature. To abide by particular ontic values is to be a particular kind of person.

Such values are logically distinct from moral, social, aesthetic and intellectual values. The latter imply criteria for determining the rectitude of actions, the authenticity of forms and the correctness and relevance of procedures. As such they do not constitute ontological relations but guide the establishment of such relations by determining the acceptability of personal behaviour. Their logical role is that of the determination of true objectivity in patterns of objective self-integration. Thus moral values play a canonical role in prescribing the correct treatment of persons as persons by persons. They do not constitute a man's spirit.

Moral, social, aesthetic and intellectual values are all reasonable in the sense that they are only acceptable in the light of

108

high-level metaphysical presuppositions. In their different ways Aristotle, Kant, the Utilitarians and the Evolutionists have all argued that certain moral qualities are desirable given, and only given, that a person is a particular kind of being. The social value of 'toleration' (of political opponents) is justifiable only in the light of some deeply held belief about the nature of society. Aesthetic values are promulgated in the light of accepted social traditions: and intellectual values of relevance, appropriateness and correctness stem from the postulation of rational goals of intellectual endeavour.

The ontic values of religion are not reasonable in this sense at all. They are not justified in the light of some other assessment of what the case is, or what is desirable: instead they are themselves the very determinants of all other values because they are regarded as being constitutive of what the case ultimately is and ought ultimately to be. They are the final stopping points in any argument of an evaluative kind because they do not possess merely canonical and regulative status but also ontological status as constitutive of man's spirit. Moreover they do not simply guide objective self-integration but constitute the ultimate object with which the individual person as self-conscious interactor may interact.

That which is spiritual and that which is ontically valuable in an ultimate sense is identical. The spiritual life of a person is the pursuit of quality: and in religious terms such quality appertains to ultimate spiritual reality. This is clearly seen, for example, in 1 John 4.7-12 with its key phrase 'God is love'. For the Christian, God is both ultimate reality and ultimate value: and so is love.

The phrase 'God is love' is a tautology, only not an empty tautology. Its significance as a religious utterance is abundant as emphasizing that the authentic spiritual (Christian) path of life is the pursuit of ontic values (love) – and this, of course, in a faithful way, not in some calculating prudential manner. The persistent misinterpretation of such statements evident in the oft-repeated insistence that such religious utterances are judgments logically dependent upon autonomous moral discourse is to be regretted. 'God is love', 'God is good', 'God is righteous' are not moral judgments of God by his people but declarations of the ontological nature of the spiritual ultimate.

Moreover they are statements of faith about those values which must be instantiated in personal action if the spiritual dimension of personal life is to flower in authentic interaction.

Such discernment of ontic values in religious understanding is central to the practical nature of this kind of insight because such understanding of personal action, or a social institution (like marriage) or an inanimate object (like a building or a machine) is always discernment relevant to the spiritual dimension of a person's life. 'To what extent does this action instantiate ontic values?'; 'In what ways may this institution aid the living out of ontic values?'; and, 'How may this object assist man in abiding by ontic values?' are religious questions because they advert to the kind of discernment necessary to spiritual fulfilment.

(v) *Depth and breadth of religious understanding* As with all kinds of understanding there is depth and breadth of religious understanding. And of educational significance is the fact that religious understanding operates at all four levels of insight indicated in chapter 4, section 4 (iv). We shall return to this point about 'educational significance' in chapter 6: here we must illustrate the four levels of religious insight.

Let us take as an example of a demonstration of religious understanding the parable of the Good Samaritan:

[A lawyer] said unto Jesus, And who is my neighbour? Jesus made answer and said, A certain man was going down from Jerusalem to Jericho; and he fell among robbers, which both stripped him and beat him, and departed, leaving him half dead. And by chance a certain priest was going down that way: and when he saw him he passed him by on the other side. And in like manner a Levite also, when he came to the place, and saw him, passed by on the other side. But a certain Samaritan, as he journeyed, came where he was: and when he saw him, he was moved with compassion, and came to him, and bound up his wounds, pouring on them oil and wine; and he set him on his own beast, and brought him to an inn, and took care of him. And on the morrow he took out two pence, and gave them to the host, and said, Take care of him; and whatsoever thou spendest more, I, when I come back again, will repay thee. Which of these three, thinkest thou, proved neighbour unto him that fell among the robbers? And he said, He that shewed mercy on him. And Jesus said unto him, Go, and do thou likewise. [Luke 10.29–37]

It may be asserted in general terms that the 'concrete' level of religious insight is the discernment of particular actions which must be done because they instantiate ontic values, rather than the discernment of the ontic values themselves. So the parable demonstrates that it is required of religious (Christian) people that they give a helping hand to anyone who is in need. And the details of the parable are such as to emphasize that what is of importance is the deed and not the agent or the recipient.

The telling of stories in which characters live out ontic values without specifically mentioning them is a regular means of provoking the concrete level of religious insight. Other means include the actual prescription of certain actions (e.g. say one's prayers, give alms, refrain from using obscene language) and sometimes the actions of a great religious figure are held up as examples (e.g. Anthony's return to Alexandria at the time of persecution; Aidan's gift of his fine horse to the poor man; Cuthbert's feats of endurance and fasting). In each case that which is understood is the necessity of behaving in certain ways, and of not behaving in other ways, if the spiritual life is to go forward. And there is no disgrace in living a religious life of faithful action at this concrete level of insight.

At the 'conceptual' level of relgious insight it is the ontic values implicit in the action which are averted to. So the parable provokes discernment at this level of insight of the ontic value of 'outgoing neighbourliness': and the religious importance of the Samaritan's particular action is perceived as stemming from his adherence to this ontic value. His actions are not good because they are efficient (and certainly they are not prudential!) but because they manifest outgoing neighbourliness. In a similar way the efficacy of a religious rite is understood at the conceptual level of insight not in terms of its

111

correct performance but in terms of the acting out of the ontic values the devotees hold dear.

Further reflection upon the parable provokes intuitions at the 'formal' level of religious insight. At this level the form, or nature of 'outgoing neighbourliness' is discerned. It is perceived as distinct from 'imposing oneself on others', for example, and from 'doing good for the sake of doing good' or 'doing one's duty'. The formal level of religious insight is always the discernment of the exact logic of the ontic value(s) which is being adverted to. Such is evident in discussions about the ontic value of 'love' in the Christian life when attention is drawn to the Greek words 'eros', 'philos' and 'agape'.

At the fourth and final level of religious insight, the 'metaphysical', there is discerned that unity of all ontic values. Thus, in the parable, 'outgoing neighbourliness' is perceived as necessarily related to 'mercy' and 'compassion': and thus there is provoked the kind of reflection which leads to the perception of the interdependence of such ontic values with others such as 'loving-kindness', 'patience', 'self-sacrifice' and 'charity'. The metaphysical level of religious insight is that at which the unity of the religious life is discerned. Moreover it is at this level of insight that the full significance of this particular parable of The Good Samaritan is grasped. Of significance here is the fact that the lawyer's question directs attention upon one's neighbour – that is, upon one of the particular objects with which one interacts. In reply Jesus redirects attention to oneself as an interactor and insists that authentic self-integrating interaction has to do with one's abiding by ontic values. At this metaphysical level of discernment it is perceived that the spiritual life is primarily a matter of the subject abiding by ontic values whatever the circumstances. In this sense religion is 'a personal matter' and not a matter of objective rites, rules, places and other people.

It is because the necessity of the subject abiding by ontic values is intuited as of prime importance at the metaphysical level of religious insight that such understanding is logically competent to discharge a function which no other kind of understanding can play without stepping outside its logical boundaries – that of unifying all insight. Any kind of perception of relations ultimately results in unifying insight: but of interest here is the fact that some kinds of intellectual discernment are factual, others procedural, and others to do with intrinsic value. The logical problem is always that of crossing the boundaries between logically distinct kinds of understanding.

It is by dint of the intuition of ontic values at the metaphysical level of insight that religious understanding enables harmonious personal self-integration by uniting facts and values. This it does by rooting all personal endeavours in ontic values because through the perception of ontic values is not only discerned what is of ultimate personal value, and what is of lasting ontological significance to a person, but at the same time there are perceived determinants of the kind of life which a person should lead. For the personal life to be harmonious there must be ultimate transcending, infinitizing, unifying ontological qualities: and it was no accident that Plato perceived ultimate reality as the Form of the Good. Such an insight was an intuition at the metaphysical level of religious understanding.

Coupled with such depth of religious understanding is breadth. And as religious understanding is always handmaid to the practice of the spiritual life so breadth of religious understanding may be formally characterized as insight into the ways in which ontic values may be lived out and promulgated – and the greater the number of ways discerned so the greater the breadth of religious understanding.

There can be little doubt that it is possible to have 'narrow' religious understanding: that is, there is spiritual insight but it is limited both in terms of insight into the possible presence of ontic values and in terms of discernment of possibilities of promoting such values. As has been argued earlier, such narrowness/breadth of understanding is necessarily related to shallowness/depth of insight. Once conceptual and formal levels of religious insight are achieved then breadth of religious understanding becomes much more possible.

Most people will recognize an ecclesiastical building or a meal as having potential in terms of the possible presence and living out of ontic values: but it takes breadth and depth of religious understanding to perceive such possibilities in say, a

113

twin-cylinder motorcycle, a public lecture or a whelk stall. That the religious dimension of life is spiritual requires no further emphasis: that the spiritual is believed to be in any way limited to particular actions by particular people on particular occasions is a narrowness of understanding firmly related to a concrete level of religious understanding. Depth and breadth of religious understanding perceives all life as potentially a field of spiritual activity.

(vi) *Criteria of logical cogency and truth*   The one thing that a fully developed religious understanding does not perceive, however, is that all life is necessarily expressive of authentic spiritual activity. Only those actions, activities and attitudes which instantiate ontic values are manifestations of authentic spiritual activity. A good many human endeavours are in fact the outworkings of deontic values: that is, they instantiate values which in fact destroy the spiritual life by severing spiritual relations of ontological dependence.

Only those qualities of life which, when pursued and believed in, enable the communion and union of the spiritual self with ultimate spiritual reality, are ontic values. The pursuit of such values which prevent such union is quite possible. No one can deny that they are values – e.g. envy, selfish rivalry, pride, conceit, contempt, cynicism – but as such they vitiate the possibility of that interaction which is the union of man with the ground of his being. As such they are regarded as deontic from a religious point of view because they threaten the very existence of the spiritual life of man.

The function of religious understanding is the discernment of those ontic values to be lived by the man of religious faith. Religious understanding is therefore no different from any other kind of intellectual understanding in being the perception of relations in conformity with criteria of logical cogency and truth. Should the outliving of a particular value having deontic quality – such as 'avarice' – be adumbrated then such is false religious insight. Understanding is always perception abiding by the truth: and religious discernment of ontic values is no different.

Those criteria of logical cogency and truth to which religious intuition must conform must therefore be characterized:

and such may be done in 'functional' and 'essential' terms. In the first place, inasmuch as religious understanding is the handmaid to the spiritual life, so it follows necessarily that the perception of relations of ontic value is correct when the believing in, and pursuit of, such values enables that continuing spiritual interaction which is the religious dimension of personal life. Now that spiritual interaction between man and the cosmos has been seen to be continuing when the life of each individual person manifests ever more clearly the features of 'freedom', 'peace' and 'justice' (cf. chapter 3: section 1 (vii)). It is therefore the case that, from a functional point of view, the intuition of ontic values is correct when the adverting to such values enables a life to be lived in which the qualities of freedom, peace and justice are manifested overall.

In 'essentialistic' terms it may be argued that discernment of ontic values is correct if, and only if, the values intuited are necessarily constitutive of ultimate spiritual reality. This must be so because inasmuch as the spiritual life of faith is one of communion and union of the self with ultimate spiritual reality so such identification is logically impossible unless those ontic values which are of the very nature of the spirit are abided by. To intuit correctly in a religious sense is to perceive accurately the authentic pattern of ontic values which constitute spiritual reality.

(vii) *Religious consciousness by way of conceptualization*   Now the clear perception of ontic values obviously necessitates a vibrant consciousness of the spiritual dimension of personal life. As with all kinds of understanding such consciousness involves the apprehension of objects by way of accurate description, and this implies the employment of categories and concepts (cf. chapter 4: section 1).

One category of religious consciousness must be that of *subjective agency*. In other, and negative terms – to think in mechanistic, evolutionary or blindly causal categories is not to think religiously. As has been argued, a logical condition of the concept of religion is an awareness of the self which is a self-consciousness of oneself as a subject. And, as a spiritual subject, the believing in and abiding by ontic values is the highest expression of any subjectivity known to man.

Nothing can be more valuable than a centre of value living a life of ontic values. Thus a fundamental category of religious apprehension is that of subjective agency. To think in 'object' terms is not to think religiously.

A second category, intimately linked with subjective agency, is that of *active being*. In so far as the function of religious practices is the intensification of life in all its abundance, so the category of 'being' is necessary in religious thinking (and such is not the case in, say, pure mathematics). But it is spiritual life which is of prime religious concern and, as 'spirit' always implies dynamic activity, so any category of 'being' which implied fossilized staticity would be inappropriate. Only the category of active being is at home in religious discourse.

The spiritual dynamism of man can be destructive as well as creative however, and not all values have ontic quality. The importance of determining ontic from deontic values in the life of the spirit implies that both *value* and *truth* are relevant categories of no small importance in religious consciousness.

These four categories are equally constitutive of moral consciousness: what helps to distinguish religious discourse from moral discourse is the employment in the former of the categories of *transcendence* and *ontological ultimacy*. It is the very employment of these two categories of thought which distinguishes perception of the ontic values of religion from that of moral values. It is only in terms of these categories that there can be any fusion of what 'is' with what is valuable. That some moral theorists claim *logical* ultimacy for one or more of the moral principles cannot be denied. But that is quite different from the *ontological* ultimacy of the ontic values intuited by religious agents.

Together with particular categories, all conceptual schemes of apprehension also include particular metaphysical beliefs. One such belief in all forms of religious apprehension is that of *the ultimate spiritual nature of all reality*. For the religious person physical, logical and psychological forms of advertence to the things of life are not unimportant: but of supreme significance are those forms of consciousness which have regard to the spiritual. Implicit in this insistence upon the inadequacy of purely empirical and rational apprehensions of man's situation

116

is the metaphysical belief that the continuing process of inter-action which constitutes the cosmos is essentially spiritual.

A second metaphysical belief implicit in all religious dis-course is that of *the freedom of the will* coupled with belief in *individual responsibility* for volitional action. Any religious con-sciousness denies that wilful action is totally determined by 'blind' causality. It always insists that spiritual agency is in no way 'programmed' in a mechanistic way and that the agent's undertakings and intentions could have been otherwise. Moreover, religious consciousness apprehends man's status as being one of either self-maintenance or of self-destruction: that is, life is believed to have a self-reflective quality whereby any subject becomes the kind of agent he is through the choices he makes. The values that any self-conscious agent adheres to, and the activities undertaken which instantiate such qualities, are regarded as necessarily ontic or deontic. Such a form of apprehension necessarily implies belief in the freedom of the will and self-responsibility.

The third metaphysical belief constitutive of religious con-sciousness is that of *cosmological unity*. The religious outlook is always that which searches for unity in communion of the self with the cosmos. And even in those religious faiths which seem to stress dualisms an understanding of such (at the formal level of insight) indicates that such dualistic conceptions are either dualisms within a unity, or dualisms whereby the ten-sion of the two terms is necessary to maintain the unity of the whole, or a dualism in which one term is a perversion or degradation of the other term. Faced with a diverse and multi-farious world of sense-perception, and distinct forms of intel-lectual apprehension and mastery, the religious consciousness apprehends that 'everything is in the hand of God' or that 'all things are Brahman'. Implicit in such an outlook is the belief in the unity of the cosmos.

(viii) *Differences between forms of religious consciousness*   These formal categories and metaphysical beliefs are present in all forms of religious consciousness: they are necessary to reli-gious consciousness. But any form of apprehension is consti-tuted not only by categories and metaphysical beliefs but also by concepts – and all are intimately related.

What is of significance here is that it is at the conceptual level, and not at the level of categories and metaphysical beliefs, that one discerns the major differences between forms of religious consciousness. This may be illustrated by reference to the three necessary and sufficient conditions of the concept of religion analysed in chapter 3. Thus, the spiritual self may be conceived as a rational soul, a non-rational soul, a divine seed, an atman, a spiritual monad, a breath, etc. The spiritual ultimacy of the cosmos may be conceived as God, Allah, the gods, the spirits, Brahma, life-forces, Logos, etc. And the openness of being necessary to communion and union of the self with ultimate spiritual reality may be conceived as a way of salvation, of submission, of co-operation, of liberation, of enlightenment, etc. In the employment of such diverse concepts lie the profound differences of disparate forms of religious consciousness.

Any form of understanding is necessarily related to the manner of apprehension of the objects to be understood. And inasmuch as differing forms of religious consciousness will entail differing apprehensions of objects, so there will occur differences between kinds of religious understanding. This is not to say that some kinds of religious understanding will perceive relations of ontic value, and other kinds of religious understanding will discern other and different relations. All kinds of religious understanding necessarily intuit relations of ontic value: but not all agree on which those values are which have ontological import, or those relations of ontological dependence which are of ultimate value.

To insist that there is only one religion in the world, or only one kind of religious understanding, is to confuse the formal conditions of the concept of 'religion', and of 'religious understanding', with the substantive nature of religious concepts and activities. Every religious faith is the outworking of ontic values: but there can be differences of discernment regarding the nature of such ontic values.

(ix) *Symbolization of religious understanding*   Implicit in all conceptual schemes, all forms of consciousness, and all manner of public demonstration of understanding and insight, is the employment of physical symbols. Here we may confidently follow Langer in her observation that 'Symbols are not proxy to their objects, but are *vehicles for the conception of objects*',[2] and may assert that without the employment of symbols there would be no consciousness by way of conceptualization such as is known to man, and no understanding. Moreover, the point argued at the end of the chapter on Intellectual Understanding must be reiterated – that without the ability to signal symbols there would be no public demonstration of understanding to deepen such consciousness.

All kinds of human understanding employ symbols: but symbols differ in function and import in different kinds of understanding. '2+2=4' is a form of symbolization quite different from Burns' 'O my Luve's like a red, red rose, That's newly sprung in June'. The nature of symbols alters subtly from one discourse to another whilst remaining 'vehicles for the conception of objects'. This being so, it is necessary to make one or two comments on religious symbols from the point of view of concern with the nature of religious understanding.

In so far as religious understanding is the perception of ontic values so the nature and function of a religious symbol is complex. First, it must be significant at all levels of insight (and this is not the case, for example, with mathematical and philosophical symbols). Second, it must signal what 'is' and at the same time instantiate ultimate value. Third, it must provoke reaction and challenge action which is of the nature of transcending, infinitizing faith. If a crude metaphor is acceptable, religious symbols always have a mongrel nature and function.

This functional complexity of the religious symbol is heightened by the nature of their substance, the spiritual. Inasmuch as the spirit is non-physical, non-rational and dynamic so any vehicle of its conceptualization is inevitably bound to be halting and indeterminate without being insignificant. There is a sense in which that which religious symbols convey always remains beyond our reach both in terms of intellectual mastery and efficacious practice. And this being so the complexity of the symbols is such as to preclude total and comprehensive analysis of their meaning. So Dupré is correct in asserting that, 'By paradoxical phrasing, distorted forms, unusual settings,

119

they warn us that we must entirely surpass the empirical appearance in order to gain access to their inexpressible content':[3] and Fawcett is right in commenting that 'They push beyond the frontiers of empirical objectivity and seek a subjective appropriation of the transcendent.'[4]

Such functional and substantive complexity is one reason for the rich diversity of religious symbolism. To attempt to reduce all religious symbolism to a few basic categories is undoubtedly rash but useful distinctions may be made between the symbolization of religious discernment in verbal terms, in non-verbal art forms and in both individual action and communal activity.

Basic to Christian discourse, for example, are terms such as God, Jesus Christ, sin, grace, reconciliation, resurrection, sacrament, etc. These are 'basic' in the sense that it is by the employment of such verbal symbols that the Christian promotes, and attempts to express, insight into particular ontic values. On the other hand, non-verbal art forms such as pictorial art, architecture, music and dance provide successive generations with pertinent stimuli and provocations. And in action and activity – in living the life of rite, prayer, worship and service – the believer is drawn into deeper and deeper insight of himself in communion with ultimate reality.

The perception of ontic values is implicit in the symbols: and it is by dint of being soaked in the symbols that religious understanding is provoked. It is not just a matter of 'learning the verbal formulae' but, as in the case of any form of intellectual understanding having as its intellectual goal a form of practice, it is a matter of 'learning by doing'. Certainly without first-hand experience of appropriate symbols it is difficult to see how any particular discourse can be mastered and any insights achieved.

2 Scholarly understanding of religion

(i) *Its intellectual goal*   With this account of religious understanding in mind we may now consider the nature of scholarly understanding of religion and, in so doing, attempt to explicate the logical relation between both kinds of comprehension.

Both religious understanding and scholarly understanding of religion are intellectual pursuits but the fundamental formal difference between them lies in the nature of their intellectual goals. Whereas religious understanding is the handmaid of religious faith and is of a practical nature, scholarly understanding of religion is entirely theoretical in its telos and intent. Religious understanding is primarily the discernment of those steps which must be taken within the spiritual dimension of life by the man of faith, which is the pursuit of ontic values. In contrast, any kind of scholarly understanding of religion attempts to achieve a theoretical explanation of religion and religious practices.

Scholarly understanding of religion focuses upon religious phenomena. And each kind of scholarly understanding of religion does this in its own terms and with regard to its own procedures of study and its own criteria of logical cogency and truth. This being so, the relations which are discerned in any kind of academic insight will necessarily be those relevant to the particular kind of scholarly understanding employed in the study of religion.

(ii) *Religious objects apprehended by the scholar* In so far as scholarly understanding of religion attempts to provide a theoretical explanation of religion as phenomenal so the object of the scholar's apprehension comprises the forms and manifestations of the spiritual life. To employ a term used in the previous section, the scholar focuses his attention upon the religious symbols in order to discern those relations which are of interest and import to his branch of scholarship.

By way of example – the theologian's understanding of religion apprehends verbal symbols: namely, those statements about God-and-the-world which religious (theistic) understanding employs to articulate part of its insight. The historian of religion has as his focus of attention past symbolic practices: that is, those events in time past in which religious believers have actively involved themselves as religious believers. The sociologist of religion is concerned with the social role-playing which instantiates religious understanding and faith. And the philosopher of religion is concerned to examine and clarify intellectually the meaning of religious statements, the

121

significant logic of religious activities, and the tests for truth and logical cogency which are applicable and applied in the life of religious faith.

In studying such religious symbols the scholar employs another form of symbolization which is appropriate to his own discipline. Whether he be theologian, historian, psychologist, sociologist, philosopher he must employ procedures and tools peculiar to the search for truth within his own branch of academic study: he must employ a form of symbolization pertinent to the furtherance of his own form of academic discourse. A scholar of religion is therefore always working with at least two distinct families of symbols: one appertaining to religious understanding, and the other inherent in his own academic discipline.

Now in so far as both forms of symbolization are constructive of, provocative of, and expressive of kinds of understanding, so scholarly understanding of religion is always a matter of 'understanding religious understanding' and not just 'understanding religious phenomena – which are intellectually inert'. As far as the scholar is concerned it is religious texts, buildings, doctrines, rituals, beliefs, judgments, actions, attitudes, language forms, traditions, organizations, etc. which are apprehended. But each of these, in their different ways, symbolizes religious insight. Figure 5.1 may help to make this clear.

(iii) *The objectivity of religious scholarship*   It is a common requirement of scholarship that it be objective study: and part of what is meant by this demand is that, as far as is humanly possible, the object studied should be regarded in its own terms. Its own nature should be respected and there should not be wished on it that which is foreign to it. So an ornithologist would be in error in expecting birds to behave in a morally responsible manner: and the botanist would be unscholarly if he disregarded the important effect upon plants of the soil in which they grow.

The fundamental way in which any scholar achieves such objectivity is by familiarizing himself thoroughly with the object he apprehends. He must be well-acquainted with it in an 'open' way so that he learns from it rather than it being

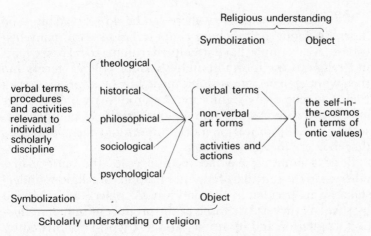

Figure 5.1   *Relationship between religious understanding and scholarly understanding of religion in terms of 'symbolization' and 'apprehended object'*

dominated by him. And the scholar of religion can be no different from any other scholar in respect of such objectivity. It is not that his understanding of religion will be shallow unless he is well-acquainted with the rich symbolization of religious understanding but that it may well be misunderstanding.

Any kind of scholarly understanding is always interpretative because the intellectual goal of scholarly understanding is the provision of coherent explanatory accounts, and not simply one of description and report. All forms of scholarly understanding, including those of religion, are forms of theorizing: and explanatory theories are always weak and erroneous when they ignore the facts of the case.

A major problem for every student of religion is that religious symbols are peculiar and particular in at least two ways. In the first place, complex religious symbols do not stand in their own right, as it were, like aesthetic symbols. The public forms and phenomena of religion are but 'empty shells' without spiritual content. Their *raison d'être* is the promotion of the spiritual dimension of life. Therefore, if these objects are to 'live' in hands of the scholar he must be sensitive to the spiritual mysteries which lie behind the tangible form.

Without such sensitivity there can be no scholarship – no 'learning about' or 'teaching about' religion. Too many historians, for example, have attempted to understand past events in a religious tradition in purely social or political terms and then wondered in cynical amusement why believers view such events as religiously significant. And too many philosophers have insisted upon studying religious utterances as either possessing only empirical or moral import and then concluded that they are logically vacuous.

Besides pointing beyond themselves to the ontic values inherent in the spiritual life, symbolizations of religious understanding are peculiar in a second way. As objects apprehended by scholars they are themselves the product of human reflection, cogitation and intuition. And in a world dominated by much crude positivistic scientism such objects of study are often misunderstood. The pure sciences constantly apprehend phenomena devoid of intellectual content or agency: but the scholar of religion apprehends phenomena which are expressive of intellectual insight and personal commitment. The scholar of religion is therefore always working at two levels: from the point of view of his own academic discipline he is indulging in 'higher-order' scholarship of 'lower-order' religious understanding. The scholarly understanding of religion is therefore always highly reflective (and very adult) for in effect it is always reasoning about reasoning about human spirituality: and that necessitates academic insight into spiritual insight.

(iv) *Depth and breadth of religious scholarship*   It goes without saying that scholarly understanding of religion may be broad and deep, or narrow and shallow. If it is to be the former then obviously the scholar must be proficient in his own academic discipline. But the point which concerns us here is that, by itself, such proficiency will be of little avail unless that same scholar has depth and breadth of religious understanding.

If, for example, a philosopher is to understand religion and religious practices, he must not only be one who has a 'nose' for a good or bad argument, who is well-versed in the logical moves and potential fallacies of his own field, and whose attitude is that of passionate concern for clarity of thought and justifiable statement but, in addition, he must have breadth and depth of religious understanding. He must be able to 'get inside' the thought forms of the religious believer, sympathetically to share the feelings of the devotee, to know what it is like to indulge in esoteric religious practices. He must be sensitive to those forms of symbolization which embrace ontic values. And if he cannot do this then it is a logical truth that his philosophical understanding of religion must necessarily remain shallow. And the same can be said of the historian, sociologist, theologian or any other scholar of religion.

It may be asserted therefore that the promotion of religious understanding is logically prior to the establishment of any deep scholarly understanding of religion. And this truth is ignored at peril by any scholar of religion or any advocate of particular approaches to, and methods of teaching, in religious education. (We shall return to this in chapter 6.) But the converse is not so: the promotion of religious insight is not logically dependent upon breadth and depth of scholarship.

One clearly observes this asymmetrical relationship between the scholarly understanding of religion and religious understanding in the early years of development of any new religious 'faith' as well as in the 'faiths' of primitive peoples. The scholarly understanding and interpretation of the Christian Faith by the Fathers came many years after the original proclamation of the ontic value of Christ crucified and risen from the dead. And in a good many 'primitive' religions there is a marked absence of such doctrine. But no one can deny the presence of religious insight.

The case is similar in the lives of many individual believers. Their religious insight may be profound: their scholarly understanding of religion almost nil. Of St Peter it has been commented that he would never have been welcome in any university common room – whether senior or junior. And the point is well made in the delightful story of Archbishop Fénelon:[5]

The saintly Fénelon, Roman Catholic Archbishop of Cambrai, finding a cow going astray brought it back to its owner, a Huguenot peasant woman. In the conversation which followed, Fénelon asked her, 'Where was your religion before Calvin?' She replied, 'Monseigneur, in hearts such as yours'.

Nobody can question the religious insight of this peasant woman but one can justifiably doubt her possession of much scholarship.

It can be said with confidence that the possession of religious understanding does not entail great depth of scholarly under-standing of religion. No one would deny that possession of the latter might assist development of the former: but it is not logically necessary. On the other hand, possession of religious insight is necessary to the establishment of scholarly under-standing of religion. The implications of this in practical terms must be worked out in chapter 6: but, before then, the possi-bility of religious insight being established in the absence of religious faith must be examined.

3 **Religious understanding without religious faith**

(i) *Religious faith requires religious understanding* That religious understanding can be provoked without the establishment of religious faith is hotly disputed by a good many people. And our argument that the employment of religious symbols pro-vokes religious insight would seem to support those who would contend such an assumption. For how could a symbolic action which is a religious action in fact be religiously signifi-cant without religious faith on the part of the agent? Are we not driven to conclude that the demonstration and promotion of religious understanding necessarily involves faithful action? Conversely, how could it be possible to indulge in any reli-giously faithful action without some religious understanding?

Such questions are of no small significance pedagogically and much ink has been spilt debating the necessity – or, immorality – of establishing some religious faith in order to promote religious understanding. And we might profitably join this debate by noting in the first instance that it seems impossible to conceive living a life of religious faith without having some religious understanding.

In so far as a person is always an intellectual subject so the

126

living of a religious life by a person is impossible without some intellectual functioning. It would be impossible for a person to indulge in religious practices as religious practices without some religious understanding – even if the level of insight be only that of the concrete level. In order to be efficaciously active one must have some insight into what one is doing. Presumably one could understand one's own activity in some erroneous way and still 'go through the motions': but in the case of religious practices this would effect a reduction of such endeavours to the categories of, say, 'magic', 'superstition' or 'social climbing'. As such, the agency would no longer be religious, even if it be faithful.

(ii) *Walter Hilton's observations*　To be religiously faithful requires some religious understanding. That is patently so. The more difficult question concerns the possibility of the provocation of religious understanding without the concurrent establishment of religious faith. In a nutshell – can one religiously understand objects without being religiously faithful?

We might begin to tackle this question by noting some remarks by as great an authority on the contemplative life of the Christian as Walter Hilton. He writes:[6]

> In the contemplative life there are three degrees. The first degree consists in knowledge of God and of spiritual matters. It is reached through the use of reason, through the teachings of others, and by study of the Holy Scriptures: it is not accompanied by feelings of devotion infused by a special gift of the Holy Spirit. Learned men and great scholars who have devoted great effort and prolonged study to the Holy Scriptures reach it to a greater or less extent as a result of natural intelligence and regular study, employing the gifts which God gives to every person who has the use of reason. This knowledge is good and may be termed a part of contemplation inasmuch as it implies perception of the truth and a knowledge of spiritual things. But it is only a figure and shadow of true contemplation because it does not bring with it any spiritual experience or inward savour of God, for

127

these graces are granted only to those who have a great love for Him. This fountain of love issues from our Lord alone, and no stranger may approach it. But knowledge of this kind is common to good and bad alike, since it can be acquired without love. Therefore it is not true contemplation, since heretics, hypocrites, and men of a worldly life are sometimes more knowledgeable than many true Christians although they do not possess this love.

These remarks by Hilton assume specific Christian beliefs and it would therefore be invalid to deduce any conclusions from them regarding all religious faiths. However, much of what he has to say has application to all theistic faiths. And we might note the following.

Hilton clearly distinguishes 'use of reason' from 'love of God'. Intellectual mastery is different from 'spiritual experience or inward savour of God'. He also insists that intellectual mastery is a product of man's own unaided efforts: but love of God is a gracious gift of God and 'this fountain of love issues from our Lord alone'. Faith is a gift of God: understanding is a product of 'prolonged study'. And, finally, Hilton insists that there is no correlation between possession of 'knowledge of God and of spiritual matters' on the one hand, and 'love for God and true contemplation' on the other.

As they stand, these distinctions by Hilton would seem to be of sufficient strength to justify the conclusion that, as far as Christianity at least is concerned, the promotion of intellectual understanding is other and apart from the establishment of faith – and the former is possible without the latter. Indeed, if Hilton is right, then the establishment of love for God is beyond any man's controlled endeavour.

There are two difficulties, however. First, our concern is the provocation of 'religious understanding' and it might be argued that the 'knowledge of God and spiritual matters' referred to by Hilton is not the same. Second, our concern is 'the establishment of faith' and Hilton is writing of the Christian's 'great love for Him [God]' – and the two are not identical (cf. chapter 2: sections 2 and 3). Accordingly it cannot be contended that, however pertinent and relevant Hilton's remarks may be, such observations conclusively establish that religious understanding may be provoked without the establishment of religious faith.

(iii) *Understanding as 'ecstatic vision'* The question remains: can there be intellectual perception without personal commitment? can one understand a practice, or a relationship, without direct self-experience of that practice or relationship? And the answer from empirical observations seems to be, 'Yes – to some extent, at least.' The task is to express this succinctly and logically.

We may begin by reiterating that any kind of intellectual understanding is the creative intuition of correct relations. It has already been argued that to understand anything is not just to regurgitate fact, or to add yet another effect to a causal chain, or simply to mouth interpretations. There is nothing mechanical or processed about the understanding. Far from being 'programmed' in any determined way the understanding is always novel in going beyond the known and the given to perceive what is new. And even if the attained insight is already grasped by other members of society its perception by the agent is always freshly creative.

In such, and by such, creative powers, the understanding is the intellectual power whereby man extends himself and his experience. There is an 'ecstatic' quality about understanding whereby discernment of relations constantly draws man 'out of himself' and his present status to a new, and for the individual person, novel environment.

The creative insight of the intellect is ecstatic foresight. It enables one to be visionary so that one anticipates a situation before one has even entered into it. By use of the inherent powers of imagination and reflection the understanding enables a person to go beyond himself and his present experience to envisage future possibilities and foreign situations.

(iv) *Understanding and experience* Understanding is always ecstatic vision: that is a first point. And a second point is that, as an interaction of each individual person with the cosmos, so understanding is provoked by confrontation with the given of life.

129

This truth is popularly expressed by asserting that one must have experience in order to understand – and the greater the experience the greater the possibility of understanding clearly. But of significance here is the fact that, simply because understanding is ecstatic vision, so the experience required need not be immediate but only relevant. One understands how something may be done, what a situation would be like, how painful an injury would be, for example, without ever experiencing such actions, situations or injuries directly, but simply by way of vision prompted by relevant perceptions and conceptions which are the result of similar experiences.

Understanding feeds on relevant experience not immediate confrontation. It is only when the given, which is to be understood, is multifarious to the point of utter dissimilarity and rabid diversity that there can be no ecstatic vision. But when there is great similarity about the varied given there can be creative intuition which is perception into the present unknown. As long as there are relevant and pertinent perceptions and conceptions then, by dint of the imaginative and reflective powers of the mind, the understanding can supersede the agent's present experience and creatively intuit relations which are beyond immediate and contemporary knowledge. And this being so, it is possible to argue that some religious understanding may be provoked without the concurrent establishment of religious faith.

(v) *Experience relevant to religious understanding*   The crux of this argument is the belief that religious faith implies a subjective agency which, whilst being esoteric, is not wholeheartedly idiosyncratic or entirely divorced from all other forms of subjective agency. That the religious dimension of life is *sui generis* and different from other dimensions of personal life is not being denied: that it is utterly unique and has no relations and similarities whatsoever with other dimensions of personal life is denied. This must now be illustrated.

Religious faith may be summarized formally as that subjective agency whereby the self is in communion with ultimate reality through the active pursuit of ontic values. As such, the religious life has similarities 'all along the line' with other dimensions of life. Faithful action, for example, is not confined to the religious dimension: again and again in rational pursuits at home and at work, in hobbies and gainful employment, we commit and involve ourselves as selves. And in our more reflective moments, when 'the busy world is hushed', we are conscious of ourselves as spiritual agents as well as mental and physical beings. Moreover, the roles we play, the inter-personal relations we enter into, and the personal relationships which 'happen' to us, give us some insight into the type of 'communion which is union'. And relations of ontological dependence and of comparative value are commonplace. We do have much experience which is relevant to the provocation of religious insight which is not directly 'religious' experience.

The weakness of the argument, however, is that it ignores that kind of transcending, infinitizing experience which, whilst being so patently present in mystical experiences, is nevertheless always present to some degree in the religious dimension of life. Might it not be argued that it is this kind of transcending experience which is of the essence of religious experience, without which all talk about 'ontic values' is meaningless because it lacks experiential 'purchase' and 'bite'? And it cannot be denied that such experience is highly relevant and pertinent to religious understanding because the percepts and concepts which constitute religious consciousness are devoid of meaning and significance without it.

Of interest here is Maslow's article 'Religious Aspects of Peak-Experiences'[7] in which the author argues that men and women do have experiences which 'are essentially ineffable (in the sense that even the best verbal phrasings are not good enough) which is also to say that they are unstructured (like Rorschach ink-blots).' Such experiences may be produced by 'sexual love, or by philosophical insights, or by athletic success, or by watching a dance performance, or by bearing a child'.

These have often been understood in a thoroughly natural-istic way but Maslow wishes to argue that such 'peak-experiences' can be 'religious experiences'. He does this by listing numerous qualities of such experiences amongst which are perception of cosmic unity and integration; perception which is ego-transcending and self-forgetful; lack of con-sciousness of space and time; fusion of fact and value; and, resolution of dichotomies, polarities and conflicts of life. He argues that

> the evidence from the peak-experiences permits us to talk about the essential, the intrinsic, the basic, the most fundamental religious or transcendent experience as a totally private and personal one which can hardly be shared (except with other 'peakers').

Whether or not one accepts Maslow's identification of 'peak-experiences' and 'religious experiences', the fact which is of importance to our concern with the provocation of religious understanding apart from the establishment of faith is that here is evidence, if any was needed, that men and women who claim no religious faith nevertheless do have transcending, infinitizing experiences. They may be brief and they may be rare – especially in a civilization devoted to the great gods of noise and bustle – but they do occur. And such 'non-religious' experiences are relevant to the acquisition of percepts and concepts inherent in a consciousness which enables the intuition of religious insights.

The argument is, then, that even where there is no religious faith, or no desire to convert to a religious faith on the part of a teacher, but where there is sufficient experience analogous to religious experience, the provocation of religious understanding is possible. The depth and breadth of such religious understanding may well be less in a person who has no religious faith compared with one who has faith – assuming equal intellectual competence. But because understanding is always an intellectual phenomenon so one of no religious faith may have more religious understanding than a believer if he is more able intellectually. So Hilton's observation echoes down the centuries – 'heretics, hypocrites, and men of a worldly life are sometimes more knowledgeable than many true Christians'.[8]

Religious understanding is the intellectual perception of ontic values in spiritual terms. As such it is of assistance to that form of subjective agency which is religious faith and is accordingly of practical import rather than primarily theoretical significance. This is no argument for the necessity of such subjective agency in the provocation of such intellectual insight, although obviously the establishment of any form of practical understanding is accelerated through involvement in relevant practices. As a form of practical understanding its public symbolization is amenable to theoretical investigation: but any academic, scholarly understanding of such public forms and manifestations is necessarily shallow without depth and breadth of religious understanding itself.

Chapter 6

Teaching religion

The chequered history of religion and morality is the main reason for the widespread desire to put them aside in favour of the more stable generalities of science. Unfortunately for this smug endeavour to view the universe as the incarnation of the commonplace, the impact of aesthetic, religious and moral notions is inescapable. They are the disrupting and energizing forces of civilization. They force mankind upwards and downwards. When their vigour abates, a slow, mild decay ensues. The concentration of attention upon matter-of-fact is the supremacy of the desert.

A. N. Whitehead: *Modes of Thought*

Introduction

We began by examining the logic of aims of religious education and argued that, however great might be the differences between different kinds of aim, the aims of all religiously educational activities implicitly refer to the general aims of religious education. In their turn the general aims must satisfy dimensional, educational and social criteria.

The examination of dimensional and educational criteria led to the conclusion that religiously educational activities are those which provoke depth and breadth of intellectual understanding *vis-à-vis* the religious dimension of personhood: that this implies promotion of a sensitivity to the intuited, non-sensational mysteries of life and provocation of discernment of ontic values which constitute a person's spirituality. Such can only be achieved if due recognition is give to the nature of the religious dimension of personhood and to the logic of understanding: and an attempt has been made to become clearer about these matters in chapters 3, 4 and 5.

It is now necessary to draw practical inferences for the teaching religion in an educational setting: and we may begin this task by noting some of the implications for all educational activities before turning in particular to religiously educational endeavours.

1   Practical implications for teaching

(i) *Two contrasting models*   Our study of 'understanding' has led to the conclusion that any thought about any matter which instantiates some developed understanding of that matter necessarily involves fluidity of movement between levels of insight. Intelligent thought in educational practice is no different. It is insufficient to think of educational activities simply in terms of particular aims and methods with particular children on particular occasions. There must also be thought on a universal scale. Thus 'model' thinking in educational efforts, on a universal scale, is just as important as obsessive concern with particulars.

This is not the place to write an historical review of all the models which have been employed in educational thinking from the time of Plato to the present. For purposes of clarity (by way of contrast), however, reference might be made to two models which are known to all members of the teaching profession who have received their training at some time since the Second World War. The first of these may be dubbed the 'horticultural' model. It is that of thinking of all educational practice in terms of the 'flowering of the child's innate potential'.

The task of the teacher requires that the sacred individuality of each child be so respected that the group be organized in such a way that each member of it may be encouraged to 'grow' at his own pace and to 'realize' his own potential. Thus competition between children is rejected as unnecessary and inconsistent, and 'formal' teaching of the whole class is perceived as infelicitous. Progress is to be measured in terms of the individual child's own development and, accordingly, public examinations which measure levels of achievement within, and across, a year group are irrelevant. The names of Montessori and Froebel are classically associated with such a model.[1]

In contrast to the 'horticultural' model of educational practice is that which deifies traditional patterns of learning and social institutions of intellectual achievement, and which insists that educational practice has to do with 'initiating' children into such traditions and social institutions. We may dub this the 'pseudo-religious' model because what is considered to be of 'ultimate concern' is not the innate potential of each child but the objective standards and public hermeneutics of the social tradition. The task of the teacher is close to that of the evangelist: in Peters' words, it is 'to try to get others on the inside of a public form of life that he shares and considers to be worthwhile': it is 'turning the eye of others outwards to what is essentially independent of persons'.[2]

Such brief summaries of two contrasting pictures of educational practice at the 'metaphysical' level of insight may be regarded as too brief to be fair representation. Indeed, it may be noted that Peters allows a place for 'horticultural' education:[3]

> In the early stages of education the emphasis on individual differences must be more marked. . . . hence the relevance of activity methods and of the model of individual growth . . . such a 'child-centred' approach is as appropriate in dealing with the backward or difficult adolescent as it is at the infant stage.

Furthermore, it may well be argued that only the pedagogue who is an out-and-out theorist, and who is insensitive to the requirements of children, ever pursues either policy with tenacious purity.

Be that as it may, it is nevertheless true that this kind of model thinking at a metaphysical level of insight does directly affect educational practice: and this being so, it is incumbent upon us to draw out the implications of our arguments for generalized thinking about 'education'.

(ii) *'Education' as 'provocation'*   If an element of sloganizing be permitted, the argument to be put forward is that education is neither 'development and growth' nor 'initiation': instead 'education is provocation'.

It it be agreed that educational activities have to do with the promotion of intellectual understanding which may aid objective self-integration: and if it is accepted that intellectual understanding is the creative intuition of correct relations: then it follows necessarily that neither the realization of innate potential nor the commitment to objective standards and criteria implicit in public traditions is sufficient for educational practice. Instead, what is required is the provocation of that appropriate interaction between the individual and the given other, whereby insights may be creatively discerned.

Education is not both self-realization and initiation (even at different times, as Peters would seem to suggest) but a matter of deliberately provoking persons of all ages to enter an interactive state of creative intuition. In terms of 'understanding' any implied dichotomy between the private and the public, the individual person and the social group, is false. To be an understanding person is to stand under the discipline of public discourse: and the social traditions of learning are the continuing associations of individual persons' insights – not in some separable diastole but in an interactive harmony.

It is the task of educational activities to provoke such a state: and such may only be *provoked* (and not engineered or arranged) simply because it is an interactive state of *creative* intuition. There is no denial of either the individual's contribution to understanding an object or of the importance of objective public criteria of correctness in such understanding, but rather the insistence that whilst both are necessary to understanding anything they are nevertheless not sufficient. Discernment of correct relations is always a matter of creation of a new 'one' because it is always theoretical unification of diverse and disparate parts. Such creation must be provoked.

To teach for understanding is not to broadcast large quantities of information: neither is it to satisfy individual likes and

137

dislikes. It is to provoke creative intuition and ecstatic fore-sight. Thus one can never simply convey understanding but only enable discernment because intellectual illumination is as much self-enlightenment as social initiation, and as much social initiation as self-enlightenment, and what the educator has to encourage is that creative leap of intuition. And this being so, at a metaphysical level of understanding educational activities, can anything be said about the implications this has for what should go on in the classroom?

(iii) *The teacher's own 'love of learning'*   In practical terms, to teach for intellectual perception of correct relations is to pro-vide for the development of the powers of the mind implicit in the understanding, and to instruct in the procedures inherent in public traditions of enquiry. So the teacher must provide for perceptual experience, concept formation, use of the imagina-tion and ratiocinative reflection by each individual child. He must instruct in the appropriate steps to be taken in any discipline whereby investigations are pushed forward and canons of truth and cogency applied. These things must be done because they are necessary to 'understanding'. But, to reiterate a point, they are not sufficient for 'understanding'. The question is, what must a teacher do to provoke that creative leap of intuition?

There can be little doubt that teaching for understanding requires skills of imaginative organization, coordination and prescient questioning which might never be required in the conveying of information or the training of repetitive skills. This implies that the educator must be a particular kind of person: his own understanding must be fully developed.

In so far as it is persons who are educated, and in so far as individual persons are the kinds of individuals they are by dint of ontological relations of a social kind, so children necessarily become understanding persons by being brought up in the company of other such persons. To the extent that children are taught by persons of developed understanding so they have the opportunity themselves to enter that interactive state of creative intuition. Conversely, to the extent that children are taught by those whose insights are shallow and narrow so they are necessarily inhibited in their opportunities to become insightful people themselves. Goldsmith's characterization of the village schoolmaster as one having a 'love of learning'[4] is highly relevant.

(iv) *The skill of 'presentation'* Such personal achievement by the teacher, however, is still insufficient: he must possess skills whereby he may provoke insight in his pupils. And the first of these is implicit in the fact noted in chapter 4, section 1 (ii) that all objects of understanding are accurate particular conceptual formulations of a descriptive nature, together with the fact stated in section 4 (vi) of that same chapter that unless the object to be understood is correctly identified, and its constituent parts laid out, it is impossible for the pattern of necessary relations which unite the parts in a whole to be discerned.

That skill which any teacher of understanding must master is therefore that of the clear and accurate presentation of the object to be understood. The skilful presentation of material necessarily aids provocation of insight into patterns of relations because it enables the correct relations to be perceived easily.

(v) *The skill of 'prescient questioning'* In harness with this first skill is a second: that of prescient questioning. Lonergan comments that 'insight depends upon an habitual orientation, upon a perpetual alertness ever asking the little question "why?" ':[5] and whilst 'why?' may not be the only question which provokes insight it is nevertheless true that insight is so often provoked by questioning. This being so, it is incumbent upon the teacher to lead his pupils to make that creative leap of intuition by means of skilful questioning. The teacher himself should know which relations (or, which kinds of relations) are to be intuited and should voice the appropriate questions which may provoke the insight.

(vi) *Pitching the level of insight* Implicit in this second skill is another ability required of the educator. Our study has led to the conclusion that there are different levels of insight: and that a fully developed understanding is one which moves easily from one level to another as and when appropriate. It follows, therefore, that in order to teach for understanding the teacher must both know and recognize the particular level(s) of insight at which his pupils may creatively discern relations. He must encourage movement from one level to another whenever appropriate.

To believe that all understanding is, say, at the 'conceptual' level, or, that the 'concrete' level of insight is unimportant, is to be profoundly mistaken. The teacher must be very clear in his own mind about the level(s) of insight at which he is working and endeavour to achieve maximum clarity of insight at each level. Only in this way can there be authentic and genuine unity of insight.

(vii) *Integrated studies*   Finally it may be noted that emphasis upon the provocation of unified insight does not necessarily entail that the kind of approaches sometimes referred to as 'inter-disciplinary studies' or 'integrated studies' are necessary.

It is clear that breadth of understanding entails depth of understanding (cf. chapter 4, section 4 (v)). But such unity of fully developed understanding does not necessarily imply that the practical steps taken to achieve it must necessarily embrace numerous logically disparate kinds of understanding at one and the same time. Unifying breadth of understanding only becomes possible at deepening levels of insight, which in turn requires clarity of insight at each level. So, at a 'concrete' level of insight the possibilities of integrating diverse and differing kinds of understanding are minimal: at the 'metaphysical' level they are maximal. This being so, in the planning of a programme of studies particular attention must be paid to the exact moment when any kind of integration is attempted.

It may often be the case that a great deal of groundwork in particular 'subject areas' at low levels of insight will have to be done before any fusion of the insights attained can be attempted. What must never be accepted as satisfactory is an attempt at integration of symbolic expression (e.g. 'power' in the sciences, political 'power', and the 'power' of the spirit) without perception of the exact relations demonstrated. The call for provocation of unity of insight is no direct justification of choice of 'integrated studies' as a method of teaching.

2   **The religiously educated person**

(i) *The primacy of spiritual insight*   Turning from more general matters to the specific task of religious education, our study leads us to observe that the prime concern of religious education is religious insight. It is the provocation of spiritual insight which is central to religious education. As the work of any educator is the provocation of insight into the condition and status of man, so that of the religious educator is particularly concerned with the spiritual dimension of personal life. He may, on occasions, advert to the moral dimension, historic dimension, aesthetic dimension or even the political dimension of life but his fundamental role is that of provoking discernment of the pursuit of ontic values.

The Psalmist's question, 'What is man?', is of major and abiding importance in all educational activities in so far as such contribute to objective self-integration. Religious education is concerned with exploration of the spiritual life of man so that children may begin to discern those relations of ontological dependence of a transcending and infinitizing nature which are of ultimate and absolute value in life.

It is the provocation of religious understanding which is central to religious education: and this, as we have seen, is other than the scholarly understanding of religion. But breadth of understanding of the spiritual dimension of life profits from scholarly understanding of religion, even if it does not necessarily require it. However, it cannot be emphasized too strongly that our argument leads us to conclude that depth and breadth of scholarly understanding of religion is logically impossible without possession of religious understanding.

Scholarly understanding of religion requires a sensitivity to, and an awareness of the implications of the advertence to ontic values which is only attained by possession of religious understanding. Any suggestion therefore, that religious education can go ahead simply and solely by dint of the examination of religious phenomena through scholarly means alone are to be rejected as impossible because they are illogical.[6]

In pursuing the provocation of religious understanding as of prime concern, religious education is only concerned with moral values, life-stances and social attitudes in so far as they encourage and enable vision of those ontic values which constitute spiritual reality. Interest in morality, ideology and cultural customs is justifiable in religious education only in so far as it provides suitable launching pads for the examination of, and consequent insight into, the spiritual self, ultimate spiritual reality and the appropriate openness of being necessary to the religious dimension of personal life.

Moral education, political education and simple sociology have no place in religious education in their own right. No one can deny their independent educational potential: but under the aegis of religious education their general aims must be subservient to that of religious education, which is primarily the provocation of spiritual insight.

(ii) *Some erroneous concepts*   The argument is, then, that the religiously educated person is one who is spiritually insightful, and this conclusion differs from other ideals which have been held up for religious educators to pursue.

Some have argued that teachers of religion should 'educate' their pupils to become members of some *'congregatio fidelium'*[7] or, at least, to have a religious faith by which to live.[8] But this is to confuse 'conversion' with 'education' (cf. chapter 2) and whilst the former salvific task may be that of the proselytizing churchman it is not that of the educator.[9] Others have suggested programmes akin to socialization rather than education – thus Cox is of the opinion that 'the test is the contribution that the subject will make to a pupil's personality or his usefulness as a workman or citizen'.[10] And others, in their turn, have implied that a religiously educated person is one who possesses much factual data about religions, or, more usually, about the scriptures of one particular religion.[11]

In contrast to such views our study leads us to conclude that a religiously educated person is one who is capable of spiritual insights as and when required, and who also has some scholarly understanding of religious phenomena. Thus, with regard to the references in the previous paragraph, it may be asserted that, whilst it is not the task of the educator to evangelize on behalf of any *congregatio fidelium*, it is his task to deepen and broaden the spiritual insight of those children who do belong to any such 'congregation' so that they may better understand their own faith, and to provoke religious discernment in other children so that should they ever consider becoming members themselves they may do so in an insightful and intelligent manner. To continue with these references – the religiously educated person is one who may perceive 'work' not simply in terms of functional instrumentalism but in the potential outworking and realization of ontic values. And the scriptural knowledge gained may not be summed up simply in terms of names of characters, lists of events and textual quotations but in terms of the ontic values to which the scriptures bear witness.

(iii) *Spiritual awareness* The religiously educated person is one who is aware of the spiritual dimension of personhood. He is at the least sensitive to spiritual matters and at the most perceptive at all levels of insight of the ramifications and implications of the spiritual for personal life. Thus the religiously educated person is one who realizes that personal fulfilment is not simply a matter of material possessions, meretricious academic advancement, social status and acceptability or political aggrandizement, but is a matter of spiritual growth and development which is to be achieved by clinging to ontic values. Moreover he is one who perceives that any kind of success is in fact no success but merely a chimera unless it conforms with that which is ontologically ultimate and objectively valuable.

In practical terms, the religiously educated person is one who is capable of assessing, say, marriage, family life, employment and recreational activities not simply in terms of economics, social parameters and individual pleasurable satisfaction but also in terms of the instantiation and outworkings of ontic values. He is capable of discerning the role of ontic values, and of advertence thereto, in the ongoing process of objective self-integration.

(iv) *Recognition of spiritual interaction* Such an ability religiously to understand the everyday affairs of human life necessarily entails that a religiously educated person is one who recognizes the spiritual when it confronts him.

Now the classic cases of such confrontation are usually those high moments in a person's life which are often unique and rare: in Maslow's terms, they are 'peak-experiences'.[12] Thus moments of outstanding success in any walk of life; occasions of significant personal involvement – such as marriage, the birth of one's first child, the death of a beloved relative or friend; and times of peace, relaxation and withdrawal from the busy world – whether walking a coastal path or fishing a placid stream or listening to great music – are all occasions when the disturbing presence of the spiritual can so impose itself upon a man that he experiences its infinitizing and transcending power.

Undoubtedly such can be both an illuminating and frightening experience but to be religiously educated is at least to recognize it for what it is and not to interpret it in some erroneous hypothesis such as physical disability or mental hallucination.

Spiritual interaction is not to be discerned only in such 'classic' moments, however: it is constantly present in the affairs of life. And the religiously educated person perceives it there also. Thus among the numerous causes which appear to drive men and women to undertake work which is dangerous, ill-paid and exhausting, and thereby apparently unrewarding, are beliefs in ontic values which may never be voiced or clearly articulated. And the causes of many psychosomatic illnesses and destructive states of depression are not only individual worries and concerns about financial problems, social relations and poor work prospects, but spiritual restlessness and emptiness whereby a person is either confused about what is of ontic value or has no belief whatsoever in anything of ontic value. The religiously educated person is one who recognizes both the significant outworking of spiritual power and, conversely, the absence of spiritual fulfilment.

(v) *Discrimination of the religious and irreligious*   Such recognition of the spiritual in life necessarily involves assessment of what is spiritually significant and pertinent and what is spiritually debasing. In other words, the religiously educated man is one who is capable of distinguishing the religious from the irreligious.

By way of example we may instance the continuing interest in the occult and the paranormal, in witchcraft and satanism, and in the use of hallucinatory drugs to induce 'transcendental' states of mind. In a good many people's minds all these are lumped together as 'religious'. And if such 'pastimes' are associated largely with the 'drop-outs' of society, or with middle class 'intelligentsia', then, amongst those who live on new large housing estates and in blocks of high-rise flats in city centres, there is the regular knocking on the door of itinerant evangelists who peddle their wares under the banner of 'religion'.

To be religiously educated is to be able to discern what is genuinely religious in all these attractions. It is to be able to perceive the presence (or, more often, the absence) of intrinsic ontic values in that which is presented. It is to be able to perceive the faithful personal commitment to ontic values distinct from the prudential grasping of allegedly salvific straws, to discern that which is spiritually fulfilling from that which is merely aesthetically pleasing, to intuit the path of self-sacrificial openness of being from the morally correct and socially accepted autonomy of selfhood. To be religiously educated is to be able to discern the religious as the religious – and the irreligious as the spiritually parasitic.

(vi) *Scholarly insight into religion*   Successful religious education is primarily the provocation of spiritual insight. It is also the provocation of scholarly understanding of religious phenomena.

The religiously educated person is one who discerns the thread of organized religion in the fabric of society, who perceives its cultural and intellectual impact upon persons as social beings, and who intuits its causal influence on tribes and nations over long periods of history. To be religiously educated is to grasp the distinct logic of religious thinking (and not to confuse it with that of, say, scientific thinking), to ascertain the power of religious practices in the maintenance of a person's psychological balance and to understand the physical symbolization of advertence to ontic values in numerous disparate forms. It is to be able to consider in an academic way religious beliefs, practices, buildings, festivals, texts, music, gestures and forms of social behaviour from the standpoint of particular scholarly disciplines. It is both to be able to think religiously about everyday affairs and to think scholarly about religious phenomena.

3 Religious education of children of all ages

(i) *The four levels of spiritual insight* This characterization of the religiously educated person in adult terms, together with the heavy emphasis upon the centrality of spiritual insight in religious education, may suggest to some that the task of religious education is only to be attempted when children have reached an age at which they are capable of mastering abstract phenomena. Such a conclusion is wrong, however, because our study of (religious) understanding gives us logical grounds for arguing that religious education is possible with children of all ages.

In common with some other kinds of understanding, religious understanding operates at all four levels of insight. Religious symbolism is so rich in perceptual forms that religious understanding at the 'concrete' level of insight is entirely possible: and religious thought of a universal nature is so common that 'formal' and 'metaphysical' levels of insight are always present, if only implicitly so. Moreover part of the very richness of religious understanding is the constant fluidity of perception from one level of spiritual insight to another: and depth of religious understanding is often manifested in the ease and facility with which a person moves in his thinking from one level to another. Indeed it is not without significance that great religious leaders, whose depth of spiritual insight cannot be questioned, have often manifested such perceptual clarity in their ability to express universal spiritual insights, at a 'metaphysical' level of insight, in perceptual terms intelligible at 'concrete' levels of religious understanding.

In one sense it may be argued that this feature of religious understanding is not merely contingent but necessarily so. If religious understanding is to fulfil its function as handmaid to

146

religious faith then it must necessarily operate at all four levels of insight.

A form of understanding which operates only at, say, 'formal' and 'metaphysical' levels can have no immediate and direct influence upon the way in which physical specimens like human beings live their lives. One sees this, for example, in the case of pure philosophy and pure mathematics: any influence they may have upon a pattern of life is indirect and incidental and, logically, only inferential. But with religious understanding the case is entirely different.

Spiritual insight at 'concrete' and 'conceptual' levels is necessary for the direction of personal life in particular, everyday affairs. And if religious understanding is to give direction to personal life in its totality – and it must do this in so far as it is spiritual – it must also operate at 'formal' and 'metaphysical' levels of insight. It is logically necessary that depth and breadth of religious understanding manifests discernment at all four levels of insight together with fluidity of movement of creative intuition from one level of insight to another.

(ii) *Provocation of spiritual insight at all levels* The central task of the religious educator is the provocation of spiritual insight at all four levels, and across all four levels, of discernment. And because the 'concrete' level of spiritual insight is possible for all young children capable of understanding anything, so religious education at this level of insight is entirely possible in the first school. Moreover, because the 'formal' and 'metaphysical' levels of spiritual insight are often so abstruse and intellectually demanding, religious education is an entirely proper undertaking with erudite sixth-formers and undergraduates.

The important point is that religious understanding does not take place simply and solely at the 'conceptual' level of insight: and any attempt to restrict religious education to this one level is doomed to failure.[13] In order to attain depth and breadth of religious understanding children must be intimately acquainted with the perceptual symbols and symbolic practices of religion at the sense-perceptual level: they must master its conceptual discourse: and they must examine personal life in the 'formal' and 'metaphysical' structure of its spiritual dimension. And they must be led to see how insights at all four levels feed and enrich each other. If this kind of programme is carried through in an appropriate way there is a massive amount of intellectual work possible with children of all ages.

If only teachers of religion would pay much greater attention to the actual level of insight at which they are working, and do all in their power to generate insights at that level, then religious education would go on apace. A great deal of work which needs to be done at the 'concrete' level of insight is often vitiated when teachers hurry on all too quickly and attempt to establish 'conceptual' insights. And once the 'conceptual' level of insight is reached – or, just confusedly approached – then this is sometimes repeated *ad nauseam* year after year to the point of boredom, and no attempt is made to provoke insights at the 'formal' and 'metaphysical' levels of spiritual insight.

(iii) *Teaching 'self-sacrifice' at the 'concrete' level*   An example may help to illustrate the points being argued. The religions of the world teach that 'self-sacrifice' is a necessary ontic value. Pure giving of oneself with no ulterior motive, no hope of gain or desire for reward, is perceived as a spiritually necessary part of living the abundant personal life. It is not a moral prescription,[14] not an aesthetically pleasing experience and not a social requirement.[15] It is advocated as something which is ontologically necessary and of ultimate value.

Such self-sacrifice is manifested in a host of stories about people who have adverted to it, in parables and myths which instantiate it, in songs and hymns which extol it, in ritual acts and actions which express it, in pictures and graphic symbols which illustrate it and in contemporary social forms which enact it.

All these are perceptual symbols of self-sacrifice and, at a purely 'concrete' level of understanding, very young children can be soaked in these symbols. They can be told the stories, encouraged to sing the songs, invited to join in ritual acts, shown the pictures which illustrate it and given the opportunity to give of themselves (their pence, very often) to assist others. And all this may be done without attempting some higher-level explanation than that of 'giving'.

(iv) *Teaching 'self-sacrifice' at the 'conceptual' level*　If this 'concrete' insight into self-sacrifice is rich and varied then the 'conceptual' level of insight becomes much more possible. The greater the breadth of experience of self-sacrifice at the 'concrete' level, the greater is the possibility of 'conceptual' insight – of being able to discern self-sacrifice as the spiritual force which has empowered a good many people to attempt the apparently impossible and to live free lives at peace with themselves – that is, as well-integrated objective self-integrators. For it is at the 'conceptual' level of insight that the instantiation of the ontic value (of self-sacrifice) is perceived as one of the necessary relations which must be intuited if the action, activity or institution is to be intelligible in a religious way.

(v) *Teaching 'self-sacrifice' at the 'formal' level*　At the 'formal' level of insight there is provoked that discernment of the exact nature of 'self-sacrifice' and of the nature of its distinctiveness from, say, altruistic involvement which is morally motivated, from self-donation which is circumscribed by self-governed criteria of competence and need, from personal involvement which is simply expedient, and from sacrifice which is heteronomously imposed upon one.

It is important to remember that the intuition of such distinctions may never occur, and that their symbolization may be mere verbiage, if the children are not encouraged to return in their thinking to 'concrete' and 'conceptual' levels of insight because the provocation of such a 'formal' level of insight into spiritual relations is necessarily that much deeper and broader if children are encouraged to perceive such distinctions in actual existential examples.[16]

Fluidity of movement between levels of insight into the ontic value of self-sacrifice is utterly necessary for full insight at any one particular level of discernment. But the provocation of such fluidity of movement between the levels of insight only becomes possible in a creative way when there is clarity of insight at each level.

(vi) *Teaching 'self-sacrifice' at the 'metaphysical' level*　Such unity of understanding is incomplete without intuition at the 'metaphysical' level of insight for here is perceived the utter necessity of the ontic value of self-sacrifice in the religious understanding of the cosmic significance of man. Faced with the mysteries of life – those non-sensational depths of personal experience – religious understanding discerns that life is only meaningful if the life lived is one of self-sacrifice.

Now it is undoubtedly a true paradox that the continuing way of objective self-integration is one of self-sacrifice and, moreover, that the ultimate ontological form of the cosmos is inherently one of self-abasement. But that this is so is undoubtedly the case: or, at least, it is undoubtedly believed to be the case by a good many people.

What is of importance here, from an educational point of view, is to note that as soon as one begins to grapple with such ideas, in order to gain clarity of insight, then philosophical considerations need to be taken into account in order to perceive both linguistic functioning of the locutions and the metaphysical implications of a cosmological order. In other words, it cannot but be observed that depth of religious insight (at the 'metaphysical' level) is only possible through breadth of insight in the sense of the insight being philosophico-religious.

(vii) *The practical significance of such religious education*   Such breadth and depth of insight is not solely philosophico-religious however. Any clarity of spiritual insight at the 'metaphysical' level also entails discernment of the intimate relation between non-rational and rational features of personhood. In the case in mind – that of the ontic value of self-sacrifice – it may be perceived that advertence to such is in no way rationally justifiable. Living a life of self-sacrifice is rather a matter of faithful commitment and not of rationally determined strategy. But the outworking of advertence to such an ontic value is nevertheless capable of being instantiated in both rational and irrational forms. And that having been said, it is obvious that epistemological, moral and social questions are already raising their heads.

Any educator who can provoke such discernments and questions in young men and women is surely to be encouraged for here is a logically sound means of provoking that unity of depth and breadth of understanding into man's condition and status which, as we have argued, is the contribution which educational activities make to objective self-integration. Thus religious education may play a central role in educational efforts.

Its educational role is further enhanced once it is realized that vibrant religious education involves the whole person as an intellectual agent. In order that depth and breadth of religious understanding may be provoked children must be encouraged to use their powers of sense perception, conceptualization, imagination and ratiocinative reflection. All powers of the mind are required for religious understanding (and this is not so in, say, philosophy and mathematics which provide little scope for sense perception) and yet they must be disciplined by reality principles (unlike, say, work in imaginative writing, some art forms and some branches of physics[17]). Indeed, one might construct a whole series of schemes of 'inter-disciplinary studies' with religiously educational activities as the lynchpin.

(viii) *Examination of religious insight*   Hand in hand with such activities goes the necessary demonstration by the children of discernment of ontic values. The most obvious manifestation of this is in internal and public school examinations: and our study of understanding has implications in this area as well.

There can be little doubt that a good many of the examinations being conducted in religious education nowadays are avowedly examinations in 'religious knowledge': and such 'knowledge' is often construed as scholarly understanding of religion. If religious education is to go ahead primarily concerned with the promotion of spiritual insight then undoubtedly examiners will have to devise new syllabuses and new examination papers concerned with the perception of ontic values.

This is not to say that questions probing the scholarly understanding of religious phenomena by pupils are irrelevant to religious education: instead, what needs to be thought out carefully is the precise import of the questioning in terms of the kind of insight and intuition which is to be elicited. And, as our examination of 'understanding' has shown, this is different in the case of religious understanding and in the case of scholarly understanding of religion.

Some examples of the kind of examination question designed to elicit evidence of spiritual insight might help to make the point a little clearer. Thus:

1 On occasions murderers are executed for their crimes. Discuss this social matter from the point of view of any one particular religion.

2 Could a Christian ever abide by the statement, 'It's my life and I'll do what I like: it's my mind and I'll think what I like'?

3 What religious beliefs might motivate an attractive woman to give up any prospects of marriage and a family and home of her own in order to care for her ailing widowed mother?

4 What considerations persuaded P (any famous 'saint' whose life the children have studied) to undertake the work he (she) did? Which of his (her) personal beliefs do you consider to be relevant to life in your own home town today?

5 A mother whose young child had been killed by a car when playing in the road was reported in the newspaper as saying, 'I won't forgive and I can't forget.' Discuss her statement from a Christian (Jewish, Moslem, Buddhist) standpoint.

6 How does the 'ideal person' depicted in advertisements differ from the Christian (Jewish, Moslem, Buddhist) concept of man?

7 Give a Christian answer to the question, 'If God is Almighty and loves us so much why does he not stop the war in (any contemporary war-zone)?'

8 Emily Dickinson once wrote,

> Parting is all we know of heaven,
> And all we need of hell.

What do you understand by the Christian (Moslem) use of the terms 'heaven' and 'hell'?

The intention of such questions is to encourage concentration on the provocation of religious understanding so that children become the kind of religiously educated person described in section 2. In most cases a particular religion has been indicated but some questions might well be framed in such a way that diverse and contrasting insights are sought in the answer.

The kind of answer sought by such questions is of the 'essay' type but a second implication for examinations in religious education consequent upon earlier thoughts is that, in so far as there is no necessary relation between the possession of understanding and its demonstration, so it would appear to be only fair to give candidates the opportunity of demonstrating their possession of understanding in more than one way. There is a field of research here for experienced, professional examiners in constructing new ways of testing children's religious understanding.[18]

A third implication for examinations arising from our study must be that examining bodies must pay great attention to the different levels of religious insight. Some examination questions may well be framed with only two levels of insight in mind – say, 'concrete' and 'conceptual', or, 'conceptual' and 'formal' but, in addition, those questions which are attempting to discover whether in fact a candidate has great depth of religious understanding must be framed in such a way that expertise in moving easily from one level of insight to another is capable of being manifested. So, in the case of the ontic value of 'charity', questions might not only be asked at the 'formal' level of insight about its nature but, in addition, examples of the charitable life might be requested thus searching out 'conceptual' and 'concrete' levels of insight: whilst questions about the ontological necessity of charity in the spiritual life would discover any 'metaphysical' spiritual insight.

4 Learning which aids the provocation of religious understanding

(i) *Direct experience of religious symbols* It has already been argued that to teach for the provocation of any leap of creative intuition is at least to provide for the development of the powers of the human mind implicit in the understanding and to instruct in the procedures inherent in public traditions of enquiry. In the light of this, one question which arises is, 'To what extent can the kinds of learning which assist the provocation of religious understanding be characterized?'

In tackling such a question it cannot be emphasized too strongly that one is not thinking about what is logically necessary to religious understanding but rather about what aids its promotion. The grasping and mastery of the kinds of learning indicated in this section is no guarantee of such promotion. These kinds of learning are but launching pads for the provocation of creative intuition. Should a teacher teach these kinds of learning and do nothing more by way of encouraging imaginative speculation and reasoned reflection to provoke perception of ontic values, then he is not teaching for religious understanding.

It was argued in the chapter on Religious understanding that it is by means of a variety of forms of symbolization that perception of ontic values central to the spiritual dimension of life is provoked, expressed and demonstrated. This being so, one kind of learning which would aid the provocation of religious insight is that acquisition of knowledge which is knowledge-by-acquaintance, or, knowledge which is direct experience of objects. It is the kind of knowledge which is beyond description in terse, succinct propositional form. It is a matter of the individual's own experience of acquaintance with, and confrontation by objects. It is certainly not something which is available second-hand.

In practical terms, what is being suggested is that religious educators give children as much experience as possible of religious symbols – and that in all the richness of their verbal, non-verbal and active forms. Children should not be confronted simply by religious texts but by religious buildings, clothes, rituals, works of art, music. They should be involved in religious practices and encouraged to meet religious persons. And if these are not available in the immediate vicinity then use of reprographic devices on a large scale is essential. Children should experience at first hand the wealth of spiritual symbolism which is sensibly perceptible.

(ii) *Being informed about the spiritual life* Besides such confrontation with perceptual symbols, children also need to be given information about the spiritual life – indeed, without this many of the physical symbols with which the children become involved will be grossly misinterpreted. Much of such information will be couched in terminology belonging to individual scholarly disciplines – e.g. theology, history, sociology, doctrine – and some of it will be in evaluative terms. Herein lies one of the big dangers for religious education: that is because these different kinds of 'language-game' are employed to convey information about spiritual symbols that it is so easy for the subject to be reduced to, say, history of religion or moral education.

What is of significance here is that the use of such 'language-games' can never be sufficient for giving information about the spiritual life. Throughout history men have had to resort to the myth, poem and parable as appropriate literary genres for conveying spiritual insight and information. There seems to be a strong belief among many teachers that it is possible to 'unpack' such 'stories' into terse propositions: but this can only often be done at the risk of transforming the spiritual insight into a moral or sociological insight. We would do well on occasions to permit religious language to operate as religious language and not to attempt to reduce it to empirical and evaluative discourse.

Much of the information given about the spiritual life will concern limited, restricted practices and minute, often-temporary detail. But one of the more important pieces of information to be conveyed is of a formal nature. It is that religious life is one of practice: but it is one of doing which is being, and not one of doing which is achieving.

In the spiritual life the path is the prize: there is nothing instrumentally advantageous in being religious. Religious insight is perception of ontic value which is held to be constitutive of personal life and not some 'bonus' to human beings. Children cannot be reminded too often that, as far as the spiritual life is concerned, 'there's nothing in it for them' – except life itself. All the information which children are instructed to retain about the spiritual life should be angled to make clear the ultimate intrinsic quality of religion: it should never be presented in such a way as to suggest any instrumental value of spiritual practices.

A second kind of information which must be given to children stems from the characterization of the religiously educated person as one who recognizes the spiritual when it confronts him (cf. section 2). Children need to be informed of the kind of experience that the transcending, infinitizing experience spiritual confrontation is. Moreover they need to be made aware that such a 'sense of the numinous' is possible on all manner of occasions and need not be confined solely to 'religious' occasions. Unless children are alerted to the possibility of such experience in an informed manner they are not being intellectually equipped potentially to understand life in its spiritual dimension.[19]

(iii) *Acquisition of skills* All the information retained about the spiritual life, and all the symbols known, is of little value unless the practical import of such is perceived. Religious understanding is practical insight not theoretical explanation: and involved in any practical endeavours are skills. If, therefore, religious insight is to be provoked, the mastery of skills may well aid such provocation.

A careful distinction must be drawn between two classes of skills. On the one hand there are what might be termed 'intellectual skills': that is, those skills which cross the boundaries of diverse human endeavours in so far as they seem to aid all kinds of intellectual understanding. William Cory (1823–92), the lyric poet and a master at Eton, drew attention to such skills when he wrote:

> You go to a great school not so much for knowledge
> as for arts and habits;
> For the habit of attention, for the art of
> expression;
> For the art of entering quickly into another person's
> thoughts;
> For the art of indicating assent or dissent in graduated
> terms;
> For the art of working out what is possible in a given
> time;
> For taste, for discrimination, for mental courage and
> soberness.

156

Such arts and habits are as much to be encouraged in religious education as in other branches of education.

Besides such intellectual skills, those skills inherent in religious practices which symbolize spiritual insight also need to be mastered as an aid to provoking such insight. In Christian terms, for example, there are skills associated with worship which are not innate but which have to be learned: and the same can be said for those of meditation in many Eastern religions. Furthermore there are skills which seem to exhibit characteristics of both 'intellectual' skills and 'religious' skills – e.g. those associated with the study of religious texts (in, say, Judaism and Islam).[20] Perhaps a good example of such a skill is that of being silent: of learning to be not just quiet, but so silent that the silence can be 'felt'. In a world as noisy as ours is this skill never comes 'naturally': it has to be learned. And its value as an aid to spiritual insight is unquestionable.

(iv) *Adoption of attitudes* The logical distinction which separates these three kinds of learning is essentially epistemological: what has been adverted to are really three kinds of knowledge. And it is by means of acquiring such knowledge that one apprehends those objects whose relations are to be intuited. But in addition to acquiring knowledge there is a fourth kind of learning which may aid the provocation of insight: and that is the adoption of attitudes. Indeed, it is common experience that if a child's attitudes to work and to those around him are all 'wrong' then his potential for intellectual insight is never realized.

Once again we must beware confusing attitudes which aid the promotion of all and any intellectual insight, and attitudes which are specifically religious. Much of Cory's remarks quoted above could, for example, be interpreted in attitudinal terms and be found applicable to much diverse intellectual insight. On the other hand there are attitudes which manifest ontic values such as reverence for life, self-sacrificial love of others and merciful pursuit of principle. Moreover, it seems to be the case that, although one can advert to attitudes in verbal locutions, most of us adopt attitudes from those we encounter manifesting such. This being so, one is driven to consider whether in fact a religious educator must necessarily manifest

157

religious attitudes so that his pupils may adopt them if they so wish.

It is difficult to perceive how any educator could fulfil his role of teaching for understanding unless he manifested attitudes which aid intellectual understanding. Moreover there seems little reason why an educator should not manifest religious attitudes so long as these do not prevent him from fulfilling his social role as a teacher. But what of the teacher who is not a religious person – who has no profound religious faith – but who wishes to engage in religious education? He cannot manifest religious attitudes because he does not have them. Can he in fact be an efficient religious educator?

The point to hold on to here is that made in the chapter on Religious Understanding – that religious understanding is possible without religious faith, and that it is possible to have experience which is relevant to the provocation of religious insights which is not directly religious experience.

Of import here is the fact that all educators are honour-bound to be vibrant moral agents. They must manifest moral attitudes. Moreover they must encourage their pupils to be moral agents. And it is this experience of the adoption of moral attitudes by pupils which aids the provocation of discernment of ontic values. Moral values and ontic values must never be confused: and moral attitudes and religious attitudes must not be identified. But their nature is such that the experiencing of one aids provocation of insight in the other dimension. This being so, the adoption of moral attitudes alone by the children in imitation of their teacher is no small aid to the provocation of religious insight.

(v) *Interdependence of all learning* These four kinds of learning which aid the provocation of spiritual insight are logically independent but this does not preclude each from 'feeding' each in promoting religious understanding of man-in-the-cosmos. Two examples might illustrate this. First, to revert to the skill of praying silently. The learning of this skill may well be facilitated by knowing the reasons why one might do this – that is, by being given information – and by experiencing moments of deep silence in public rituals, in religious buildings and in fine music. Furthermore, such a skill can never be mastered unless attitudes of respect, which border on reverence, and being attentive are adopted.

The second example stems from the fact that the meaningful use of language is not independent of human situations. It is a commonplace assurance nowadays that if one is to grasp the significance of what is being said then the 'stream of life' in which the utterance is being made (of which the utterance is a part) must be taken into account. This being accepted, one may observe that religious language is no different from any other kind of language in this respect. And this being so, if we wish children to be able to employ such language pertinently – if we wish them to 'get inside' spiritual concepts – then it is logically fatuous to deny them the richness of learning encompassed by the four kinds of learning mentioned. Each of these kinds of learning provides material for introducing children to religious situations, and without such an introduction the possibility of people being able to use religious language as an aid to the provocation of spiritual insight is minimal.[21]

(vi) *The primacy of experience* Finally there arises the practical question of whether any one of these four kinds of learning is fundamentally important from a pedagogical point of view. Is there any one kind of learning which provides a logically sound starting point? And the answer appears to be that 'knowledge by acquaintance' is such a kind of learning – that children need to be given many opportunities of direct sense-experience of perceptual religious symbols, and this whatever the age. The arguments justifying such an answer are two in number.

First, it may be argued that inherent in all forms of propositional and procedural knowledge there is this knowledge of acquaintance which, at its best, is union with the object. In the case of propositional knowledge – to advert to, or to consider any proposition as a proposition necessitates some mastery of the conceptual scheme implicit in the formulation of the proposition. This, as has been argued in chapter 4, section 1 implies a knowledge of the tongue in which the proposition is couched and expressed. Such familiarity is that knowledge of language which is not a matter of propositional mastery (otherwise one enters into an infinite regress) or simply a matter of skill. Instead such knowledge is the kind of direct acquaintance whereby the very language becomes part of the person in such a way that it is 'his' language and an important and necessary means of his own objective self-integration.

It cannot be emphasized too strongly that the quality of direct, or, at least relevant, experience of an object is massively contributory, if not logically essential, to the possession of both propositional and procedural knowledge of any kind. This is consequent upon the kind of beings which persons are. Intellectual learning is not something which can go on successfully in isolation from other personal dimensions and phenomena: and the practice of any one skill is not isolable either from other aspects of individual personal life or from one's social and cosmic environs. And to think that propositions may be known and skills mastered without any relevant experience is false. In Hamlyn's words, 'a necessary condition of being said to know X is that one should know through experience what it is to stand in appropriate relations to things of the kind that X is'.[22] And certainly one will never come to adopt attitudes from other persons unless one meets such persons either in the flesh or by means of reprographic devices.

The second argument for the primacy of 'knowledge by acquaintance' as a methodological starting-point stems from our assertion that there are four levels of insight. Now in so far as to move from intellectual puzzlement to developed understanding is first to apprehend the object to be understood and, second, to acquire at first a low level of insight, so in the case of religious understanding a great deal of acquaintance with sense-perceptible religious symbols is necessary for the establishment of any 'concrete' level of spiritual insight. (In an analogous way, it may be noted that, ever since the time of Socrates, philosophical understanding at a 'formal' level of insight has often only got going by advertence to examples from experience at the 'conceptual' level of insight.) Moreover, in so far as fully developed religious understanding necessarily moves through all levels of insight, so the 'concrete' level of spiritual insight is just as important as the other three levels. And such requires direct experience of the physical symbols of religion.

We may therefore argue that a requirement of efficient religious education with children and adults of all ages is the constant confrontation of students with religious symbols so that these may be experienced at first hand. To take children on visits to religious buildings, to encourage them to join in religious rites, to listen to religious music, smell incense burning, wear vestments, spin prayer wheels, light candles, read scriptures and engage in any of the hundreds of sense-perceptible activities associated with religion and being religious is not therefore to add pedagogic frills to the central work of the classroom. It is to present them with the opportunities necessary to their experiencing forms of the religious life without which spiritual insight remains narrow and muddied and as much religious misunderstanding as understanding is provoked.

5 Some possible objections to such a programme of learning

(i) *That it is conversional* At the risk of being repetitive it must be reiterated that the argument is not that these four kinds of learning are logically necessary to spiritual insight, in the strict sense of 'logical entailment', but rather that through them religious consciousness may be awakened, religious concepts may be grasped, and the religious apprehension of objects may be facilitated, thus aiding the provocation of spiritual insight.

It must be admitted, however, that the advocacy of such a programme of learning for religious education undoubtedly raises a problem which many will feel acutely. It may be stated thus: 'Is not the pursuance of these four kinds of learning akin to the induction of young children, and the conversion of adolescent children, to some particular religious faith?' If one is not simply giving children scholarly information about Christianity, Islam, Judaism, Buddhism, Hinduism and many other 'world religions' but also encouraging them to try out religious skills for themselves, adopt religious and moral attitudes, and have first-hand experience of religious objects is this not tantamount to induction and conversion to a religious faith?

In considering this question the experience of those who have had the pleasure of teaching religion in county schools cannot be gainsaid: and it is that the possibility of slipping easily from educational activities to those which encourage induction or conversion is very real. The move from intellectual perception of relations to subjective agency in any dimension of personal life is an existential fact and Hilton's observation, recorded in the chapter on Religious understanding, that 'the use of reason, the teaching of others and the study of the Holy Scriptures' may be the first step in the contemplative life of the Christian cannot be denied.

Educational activities and agency-establishing activities are logically dissimilar but existentially very close: and just as the teacher of political history is conscious of the possibility of teaching in such a way that he may encourage membership of a particular political party, so likewise the teacher of religion is conscious of his opportunities to 'teach for faith'.

The opportunity to do something, however, is never any justification in itself of taking action, and the task of the religious educator is the provocation of spiritual insight and not the establishment of religious faith. And it cannot be argued that his task is impossible without the establishment of some religious faith. It has already been shown (in chapter 5, section 3) that intellectual perception and subjective agency are logically distinct and that the promotion of spiritual insight is possible in the absence of religious faith.

Although the pursuit of these four kinds of learning may be a first step towards the religious life it is not necessarily so. Much will depend upon the professional intent of each teacher: but the acceptable role of the religious educator must always be the provocation of religious understanding whether or not religious faith is, or is ever likely to be, established. The teacher-who-is-an-educator is not an evangelist.[23]

It may also be noted that, according to the beliefs of some theistic religions, religious faith is a gift of God and not an attainment of man. If this is accepted them obviously it is beyond the endeavours of any teacher to establish theistic faith. However, within such religious traditions one finds the belief that such a gift can only be received by those who 'put themselves in the way of God' and a teacher might very well encourage his children to do this. Once again it may be observed that such is not the task of the educator. To employ traditional terms, education is concerned with the illumination of the mind and not the salvation of souls.

The logic of this argument may well fail to convince critics of such a programme of learning in religion and the empirical point may be made that the pursuance of these four kinds of learning – even with the best of educational intentions – may in fact quite likely lead to religious faith in either the short or the long run.

If this empirical fact could be verified then it is more than likely that a good many religious evangelists would wholeheartedly support the advocacy of such a programme of learning and a good many anti-religious humanists would oppose it. But the truth of the contention is highly dubious. Many a child has been brought up in ways similar to this and rejected God in adult life: and others have come to know and love God in adult life by quite different paths. The evidence to support the contention that there is a cause–effect relation between pursuing these four kinds of learning and establishing religious faith is insufficient and unconvincing.

(ii) *That it is indoctrinatory*   A slightly different criticism of such a programme of learning might be that it is indoctrinatory. Of interest here is the fact that there seems to be general agreement that 'indoctrinatory activities' are essentially different from, and opposed to, 'educational activities'. Unfortunately all agreement seems to end at this point for there is much debate about whether 'indoctrination' refers to the end-results of a series of processes (whether an *accidental* end-result or not), the intentions of the practitioner (even if he is unsuccessful), the content of the lessons, or the particular methods which are employed. The difficulty in rebutting a charge of 'indoctrination' is therefore basically one of knowing which of these alternative meanings is implied.[24] But in one sense that does not matter as any one of these may be answered in the case of the programme advocated here for religious education.

163

If indoctrination has to do with 'unhappy' end-results which may, or may not come about whereby people are 'closed' in their minds to rational considerations then one might almost cease all educational efforts. The fact is that the best of educators often fail to achieve their goals because of circumstances beyond their control: and to condemn them for such is quite unjust. Moreover, to dismiss their work as thereby indoctrinatory would be derisory if it were not so serious. No religious educator who pursues the above programme can be accused of being indoctrinatory simply on the grounds that some of his children may become narrow-minded irreligious bigots.

This first rebuttal of one charge of indoctrination is reinforced when it is borne in mind that the intention of those who would follow the above programme is that of enabling people to achieve the greatest possible depth and breadth of spiritual insight: and this as a contribution to objective self-integration. The intention of this programme is therefore utterly worthy in educational terms and if indoctrination has to do with the practitioner's intentions then a religious educator in the sense intimated throughout this work stands acquitted of any such charge.

In terms of 'content' the charge would appear to be that religious education purveys doctrines which are highly questionable both in terms of their meaning and of their truth value. And it cannot be denied that religious utterances have received a great deal of attention from linguistic philosophers: and that those who have adopted empiricistic criteria of verification have concluded that spiritual locutions are necessarily non-sensible. One would hardly expect any other conclusion given the presuppositions.

What tends to be forgotten is both that there are truth criteria within religious discourse (it is not the case that 'anything goes') and that a good many moral, aesthetic and historical judgments likewise present similar logical difficulties. To isolate religious education, and to label it alone as indoctrinatory on the grounds that spiritual insights are logically complex and difficult to verify, is to exhibit a fanatical form of ideological selectivity unworthy of anyone who preaches objective rationality.[25]

Finally, in terms of 'methods', the programme of learning suggested for religious education can never be dubbed indoctrinatory. Such use of the term usually implies a series of processes (sometimes termed 'brain-washing') of such a cruel kind that a 'captive' finds security in his 'captors' only by coming to share beliefs held by the latter. Thus the beliefs are held on grounds of personal, or communal, authority and the indoctrination consists of the employment of particular methods to persuade people to accept such authoritative beliefs.

Such methods can have no place in the provocation of any kind of understanding, including religious understanding, for two reasons. First, they preclude any advertence to objective public criteria for the assessment of the correctness and accuracy of the purported insight. Instead they imply that that which is correct is that which is socially acceptable and psychologically reassuring. In so doing they stultify objective truth-seeking and thereby prevent intuition of correct and necessary relations. Indeed, the only relations which are permitted to be perceived are those which are dictated by those in power.

Such methods also cripple the possibility of creative intuition both by means of denying true freedom of thought and by means of psychological terror. To creatively intuit any relation is always a hazardous occupation because one may be wrong: and indoctrinatory methods are deliberately designed to punish when one is 'wrong' – i.e., when one disagrees with one's 'captors'. In this way 'captives' are psychologically conditioned to repress the creative powers of their intellect in the interests of personal safety and so understanding hardly gets off the ground.

These indoctrinatory methods are designed to promote belief in 'acceptable' dispositions (not, 'understanding') together with commitment to particular patterns of objective self-integration. The employment of such methods could not provoke authentic spiritual insights and any programme, such as that advocated, designed to do just that cannot therefore be indoctrinatory in methodological terms.

The unjustifiable charge that religious education is indoctrinatory is to be vehemently rejected. To deny children the possibility of being religiously educated is necessarily to limit their future freedom of action because it is to prevent them as adults from making up their own minds for themselves in an informed, sensitive and insightful manner. It is in fact *not* to educate children but so to limit the possibility of them becoming autonomous agents in the spiritual realm of life that one thereby necessarily attempts to socialize them into becoming either irreligious or non-religious humanists in a necessarily secular society. Such determination of the limitation of personal life and experience is a debasement of personal agency and is itself a reprehensible form of indoctrination. The moral propriety of educational activity resides in the contribution which it makes to personal autonomy, to objective self-integration, and to label religious education unfairly as 'indoctrination', and thereby to campaign for its removal from an educational curriculum, is to embrace a form of socialization which is itself indoctrinatory. And that is morally irresponsible.

6   The justification of religious education

It has already been argued that whatever is educational is primarily that which contributes to the advancement of the intellect in the part it plays in objective self-integration.

Now the degree to which educational activities may aid a person's objective self-integration is necessarily correlative with the depth and breadth of understanding attained. Shallow understanding which masquerades as developed understanding often leads to misunderstanding: extensive and clear insight, however, entails a unity of intellectual endeavour. And such discernment is obviously advantageous to objective self-integration. This being so, it may now be argued that religious education is not simply justifiable as part of an educational curriculum but centrally necessary to it.

Such an argument is only valid if it is clearly understood from the outset that educational activities are *not* concerned with the promotion of any one particular pattern of objective self-integration but primarily with intellectual advancement which aids objective self-integration: and that religious education is primarily the provocation of spiritual insights and scholarly understanding of religious faith. And these suppositions being accepted, it follows necessarily that religious education is centrally necessary to all educational endeavours for two reasons.

First, to be an understanding person is to have unified insight: it is clearly to perceive relations both within and between diverse phenomena. And of importance here is the classical distinction between quantity and quality, fact and value, because unified insight is not simply and solely discernment of what the case is but also estimation of importance and significance in terms of gradations of value. To intuit relations on a universal scale is not simply to cross the great divide between 'is' and 'ought' but to view their distinctions transcendently in a new whole.

Purely empirical (scientific) studies on the one hand, and moral, aesthetic, instrumental outlooks on the other hand, can never embrace both the ontological and evaluative-prescriptive at one and the same time. Yet such is necessary for depth and breadth (for unity) of understanding. Only the perception of those values which are ontologically necessary, together with the discernment of those states of affairs which are supremely valuable – the one identified with the other – is capable of providing the logical lynchpin whereby all human understanding may be one. And as we have seen it is religious understanding which is this very intuition of ontic values. It follows that the possession of religious understanding does not simply aid the provocation of depth and breadth of understanding but is rather logically necessary to its creation.

This first reason for the central importance of religious education in all educational efforts stems from the logic of 'understanding' as 'unified intuition of relations'. The second reason, on the other hand, stems from the nature of persons, and from the fact that educational efforts are those which aid objective self-integration.

To be a person is to be a subject-object, an autonomous-heteronomous being, an individual whose ontology is essentially social. True personhood has to do with a high degree of union and communion between the individual subject and the many objects (some of which are other subjects) with which each interacts. Perhaps the highest form of such independent dependence known to man is that observed in personal relationships, especially those of love. If educational activities are to aid objective self-integration then obviously they must say something very pertinent to such inter-actions.

Of significance to our argument is the fact that such interactions can never be purely of a physical character and need not be of a moral or mental homogeneity. We may not share all our loved one's interests, beliefs and pastimes: we may disagree over moral decisions and political ideology: but where we do find agreement is in the spiritual dimension of life. Our natures coalesce sufficiently for us to be united because we hold sufficient ontic values in common to enable us to be in deep and significant communion.

No other kind of interaction is so important for the individual person as personal communion which is union because no form of prehension is so valuable as two centres of objective valuing interacting freely and self-consciously. And if educational activities are to aid objective self-integration then they must advert to those ontic values whereby persons may achieve their zenith as subject-objects by consciously interacting with other subject-objects by dint of perusal of ontic values. And the awakening of children to consciousness of, and insight into, ontic values is the task of religious education.

Educational activities have to do with that which is uniquely personal. Unlike training, socializing, conditioning or indoctrinating, education can have no concern with limited ends (such as role-playing) but must advert to a centre of consciousness whose self-consciousness is potentially infinite, whose creativity is powerful, and whose subjectivity is ultimately a matter of faithful commitment. In other words, education has to do with persons who are in depth spiritual beings whose objective self-integration is a matter of spiritual fulfilment if it is anything.

An 'educational' curriculum which ignores the spiritual dimension of personhood is incomplete and is necessarily fragmentary and potentially fragmenting. It must include the provocation of spiritual insights which is the discernment of ontic values. Religious education is in fact neither a luxury to be jettisoned at a time of economic crisis nor a 'fringe' subject to be taught solely by the lowest paid, least experienced probationary teacher but is logically central to all educational activities.

Notes

Chapter 1: Aims of religious education

1 Cf. R. S. Peters, *Ethics and Education*, Allen & Unwin, 1966, chapter 1; and R. S. Downie, E. M. Loudfoot and E. Telfer, *Education and Personal Relationships*, Methuen, 1974.
2 R. S. Peters, 'Farewell to Aims?' in *London Educational Review*, vol. 2, no. 3, University of London Institute of Education.
3 Schools Council Working Paper 36, *Religious Education in Secondary Schools*, Evans/Methuen Educational, 1971, p.21.
4 West Riding Agreed Syllabus, *Suggestions for Religious Education*, 1966, pp.8 and 37 respectively.
5 By way of example of such confusion cf. the booklet *Objective, Fair and Balanced*, sub-titled 'A new law for religious education', British Humanist Association, Autumn 1975.

Chapter 2 Education, conversion and edification

1 M. Cruickshank, *Church and State in English Education*, Macmillan, 1964, p.73.
2 *Ibid.*, p.71.
3 University of Sheffield Institute of Education, *Religious Education in Secondary Schools*, Nelson, 1961.
4 *Children and Their Primary Schools*, HMSO, 1966.
5 R. Descartes, *Discourse on Method*, trans. F. E. Sutcliffe, Penguin Books, 1968, discourse 4.
6 E.g. G. Ryle, *The Concept of Mind*, Penguin Books, 1966.
7 W. Temple, *Nature, Man and God*, Macmillan, 1953, pp.186 and 189.

8   Quoted by E. Fromm and R. Xirau (eds.), *The Nature of Man*, Macmillan, 1968, p.69.

9   Cf. D. M. Emmett, *Whitehead's Philosophy of Organism*, Macmillan, 1932.

10   J. Oman, *Grace and Personality*, Fontana, 1960, p.63.

11   *Ibid.*, p.64.

12   H. Ishiguro, 'A Person's Future and the Mind–Body Problem' in W. Mays and S. C. Brown (eds.), *Linguistic Analysis and Phenomenology*, Macmillan, 1972.

13   Cf. W. James, *The Varieties of Religious Experience*, Fontana, 1960, chapter 9, p.203, and his remark, 'conversion is in its essence a normal adolescent phenomenon.'

14   J. H. Newman, *A Grammar of Assent*, Longmans, 1891.

15   For a view which distinguishes a 'primitive' from a 'sophisticated' concept of 'education' cf. P. H. Hirst, 'Christian Education: a Contradiction in Terms' in *Learning for Living*, Student Christian Movement, March 1972.

16   St Paul, *Galatians* 2:20.

17   *The Cloud of Unknowing*, trans. C. Wolters, Penguin Books, 1961, chapter 6.

18   James 1:27.

19   Recorded by E. Vipont, *The High Way*, Oxford University Press, 1957, p. 66.

20   W. E. C. Andersen, 'An Analysis of the Concept "Person" in Educational Theory', PhD thesis submitted to University of London, 1973.

21   By way of contrast cf. Langford's argument that 'to become educated is to learn to be a person' in his essay 'The Concept of Education' in G. Langford and D. J. O'Connor, *New Essays in the Philosophy of Education*, Routledge & Kegan Paul, 1973.

22   Cf. R. S. Peters, *Ethics and Education*, Allen & Unwin, 1966.

Chapter 3   The religious dimension of personal life

1   Herein lies a fundamental difference between the particular theory of religious education being put forward and that, for example, in Schools Council Working Paper 36, *Religious Education in Secondary Schools*, Evans/Methuen, or M. Grimmitt, *What Can I Do in RE?*, Mayhew-McGrimmon, 1973, both of which assume Professor Smart's analysis of the concept of 'religion' which is a phenomenological description of overtly observable organized religious faiths, or communities. Cf. N. Smart, *Secular Education and the Logic of Religion*, Faber & Faber, 1968.

In effect, any theory of religious education based on Smart's thought reduces religious education to academic, scholarly study of the phenomena of organized religion. Such may well be an acceptable programme in universities: but it is not religious education of children.

2 Bhikshu, Sangharakshita, *The Three Jewels*, Anchor Books, 1970, p. 56.

3 Cf. John 3:8.

4 Cf. E. L. Mascall, *The Openness of Being*, Dalton, Longman & Todd, 1971.

5 Cf. P. L. Berger, *A Rumour of Angels*, Allen Lane the Penguin Press, 1970.

6 Cf. P. R. Clifford, *Interpreting Human Experience*, Collins 1971, p. 208.

7 T. à Kempis, *The Imitation of Christ*, trans. L. Sherley-Price, Penguin Books, 1952, bk 3. 48.

8 St Augustine, *The Confessions*, trans. R. Warner, Mentor-Omega Books, 1963, bk 1.1.

9 A. N. Whitehead, *Religion in the Making*, Cambridge University Press, 1927, p.9.

10 J. Bowker, *The Sense of God*, Clarendon Press, 1973, p.72.

11 Whitehead, *op.cit.*, p.110.

12 It is this transcendence of the religious dimension of personal life which is the logical nub of any argument favouring 'implicit RE'.

13 R. Otto, *The Idea of the Holy*, trans. J. W. Harvey, Penguin Books, 1959, p.25.

14 An interesting exercise with older children is to face the question, 'Was Jesus a good man?'

15 Cf. J. W. D. Smith, *Religion and Secular Education*, St Andrew Press, 1975, esp. chapter 5 and the penultimate paragraph of the book.

16 L. Feuerbach, *The Essence of Christianity*, trans. G. Eliot, Harper, 1957, p.2.

17 *Ibid.*

18 St Augustine, *op.cit.*, bk 8.10 and 11.

19 P. Teilhard de Chardin, *Le Milieu Divin*, Fontana, 1964, p.77.

20 W. Temple, *Nature, Man and God*, Macmillan, 1953, cf. p.345.

21 Teilhard de Chardin, *op.cit.*, p.77.

22 J. Bowker, *op.cit.*, p.64. Cf. also Matthew Arnold's poem 'Dover Beach'.

23 A. Kempis, *op.cit.*, bk 3.48.

24 S. Freud, *The Future of an Illusion*, Hogarth Press, 1962, p.26.

25 Petronius, *Fragments*, no.76.
26 P. Tillich, *Systematic Theology*, Nisbet, 1964, vol. 3, p.169.
27 A. H. Maslow, *Religious Aspects of Peak-Experiences* in W. A. Sadler Jr (ed.), *Personality and Religion*, Student Christian Movement, 1970; Otto, *op.cit.*, p.160; H. D. Lewis, *Our Experience of God*, Allen & Unwin, 1959, p.112; Berger, *op. cit.,* p.118.
28 Temple, *op.cit.*, p.26.
29 A. Kempis, *op.cit.*, bk 3.39.
30 *Ibid.*, bk 2.6.
31 Whitehead, *op.cit.*, p.6.
32 S. Kierkegaard, *Concluding Unscientific Postscript*, trans. D. F. Swenson and W. Lowrie, Princeton University Press, 1944, p. 365.
33 This, really, is the nub of the problem surrounding the current Birmingham Agreed Syllabus of Religious Education.

Chapter 4 Intellectual understanding

1 D. L. Pole, 'Understanding – A Psychical Process', *Proceedings of the Aristotelian Society*, 1959–60, vol.60.
2 J. R. Martin, *Explaining, Understanding and Teaching*, McGraw-Hill, 1970, p.155.
3 L. Wittgenstein, *Philosophical Investigations*, trans. G. E. M. Anscombe, Blackwell, 1968, 1.19,23,241.
4 *Ibid.*, 1.525.
5 *Ibid.*, 1.527.
6 P. Ziff, *Understanding Understanding*, Cornell University Press, 1972, p.127.
7 *Ibid.*, pp.137 and 140.
8 A. N. Whitehead, *Adventures of Ideas*, Cambridge University Press, 1933, p.47.
9 C. Hartshorne, *Creative Synthesis and Philosophic Method*, Student Christian Movement, 1970, p.3.
10 Whitehead, *op.cit.*, pp.67–8.
11 Perhaps this is the reason why 'God' and 'Unidentified Flying Objects' are unintelligible to man.
12 Cf. Martin, *op.cit.*, p.154.
13 A. N. Whitehead, *Modes of Thought*, Cambridge University Press, 1938, p.71.
14 B. J. F. Lonergan, *Insight*, Longmans, 1957, p.19.
15 S. Toulmin, *Human Understanding*, Clarendon Press, 1972, vol.1.

16   R. Descartes, *Discourse on Method*, trans. F. E. Sutcliffe, Penguin Books, 1968, Sixth Meditation.

Chapter 5   Religious understanding

1   Cf. H. A. Williams, *True Resurrection*, Mitchell Beazley, 1972.
2   S. K. Langer, *Philosophy in a New Key*, Harvard University Press, 1963, p.61.
3   L. Dupré, *The Other Dimension*, Doubleday, 1972, p.164.
4   T. Fawcett, *The Symbolic Language of Religion*, Student Christian Movement, 1970, p.30.
5   H. D. A. Major, quoted by E. Vipont, *The High Way*, Oxford University Press, 1957, p.53.
6   W. Hilton, *The Ladder of Perfection*, trans. L. Sherley-Price, Penguin Books, 1957, chapter 4.
7   A. H. Maslow, 'Religious Aspects of Peak-Experiences' in W. A. Sadler Jr. (ed.) *Personality and Religion*, Student Christian Movement, 1970.
8   Hilton, *op.cit.*

Chapter 6   Teaching religion

1   Cf. H. Entwistle, *Child-centred Education*, Methuen, 1970.
2   R. S. Peters, *Education as Initiation*, Evans, 1964, pp.38 and 40.
3   *Ibid.*, p.39.
4   Yet he was kind, or if severe in aught,
         The love he bore to learning was in fault;
              O. Goldsmith, *The Deserted Village*, lines 205–6.
5   B. J. F. Lonergan, *Insight*, Longmans, 1957, p.5.
6   Cf. R. F. Dearden, *The Philosophy of Primary Education*, Routledge & Kegan Paul, 1968, pp.56–8, 78, 89 and 140; the evidence of the British Humanist Association in *The Fourth R*, Society for Promoting Christian Knowledge, 1970, pp.326–9.
7   By way of one example cf. University of Sheffield Institute of Education, *Religious Education in Secondary Schools*, Nelson, 1961, especially p.14: 'The teacher's weekly contacts with the children in his charge should be stepping stones on the way to this total committal of each boy or girl to God.'
8   Cf. Central Advisory Council for Education, *Children and Their Primary Schools*, HMSO, 1967, vol.i, pp.203–9.
9   Cf. T. Copley and D. Easton, *What They Never Told You About RE*, Student Christian Movement, 1974, pp.55–8.

10   E. Cox, *Changing Aims in Religious Education*, Routledge & Kegan Paul, 1966, p.53.

11   Cf. H. Loukes, *New Ground in Christian Education*, Student Christian Movement, 1965, especially chapter 3.

12   A. H. Maslow, 'Religious Aspects of Peak-Experiences' in W. A. Sadler Jr (ed.), *Personality and Religion*, Student Christian Movement, 1970.

13   This, surely, has been the failure of RE in the last fifteen years consequent upon dominant psychological research into children's religious thinking at a conceptual level.

14   'The utilitarian morality does recognise in human beings the power of sacrificing their own greatest good for the good of others. It only refuses to admit that the sacrifice is itself good.' J. S. Mill, *Utilitarianism*, Dent, 1972, pp.15–16.

15   Cf. the honours heaped on those who sacrifice themselves for society – an incongruous act if self-sacrifice is a social duty and requirement.

16   Cf. R. Pearce, *Ideas*, H. E. Walter, 1973.

17   For a discussion of the 'reality' of theoretical work in physics, cf. H. Born, *The Born-Einstein Letters*, Macmillan, 1971.

18   Cf. W. N. Greenwood and H. W. Marratt, *New Objective Tests in Religious Studies*, Hodder, 1977.

19   Regarding the occurrence of such experience cf. two books by M. Paffard, *Inglorious Wordsworths*, Hodder & Stoughton, 1973; *The Unattended Moment*, Student Christian Movement, 1976.

20   Cf. S. Weil, 'Reflections on the right use of school studies with a view to the love of God' in *Waiting on God*, Fontana, 1959.

21   It is not without significance that the first chapter of I. T. Ramsey, *Religious Language*, Student Christian Movement, 1969, deals with the nature of a religious situation.

22   D. Hamlyn, 'Person-Perception and Understanding' in T. Mischel (ed.), *Understanding Other Persons*, Blackwell, 1974.

23   Copley and Easton, *op. cit.*

24   Cf. I. A. Snook, *The Concept of Indoctrination*, Routledge & Kegan Paul, 1972; *Indoctrination and Education*, Routledge & Kegan Paul, 1972.

25   Cf. Dearden, *op. cit.*, and my own article, 'An Examination of Dearden's Arguments on Religious Education', in *Learning for Living*, Student Christian Movement, May 1970.

Name index

Subject index

Academic work: beauty of, 31; scholarship, 120f, 145; understanding, 43

Activities: educational, 2, 7, 9, 41, 42f, 46, 64f, 137, 162, 168; logic of, 2, 80

Allah, 25, 118

Autonomy of persons, 30f, 35, 41, 58, 62f, 166

Brahman, 118

Buddhism, 40, 63, 161

Children, 7, 8, 10, 23f, 37f, 135f, 146f, 154f

Christian: Church, 23; education, 24; religion, 6, 38, 109f, 127, 161

Concepts: analysis of, 46f; evaluative, 5; formulations, 69f, 77; possession, 72, 97; religious categories, 115f

Consciousness: public features of, 68f, 73; religious, 115f; self-consciousness, 26, 32, 51f, 56f, 68f, 168

Creativity: a category, 34; in interaction, 73f, 130, 137

Dimensions of personal life: mental, 25f, 68f; ontological dependence, 82, 107f, 138; physical, 27f; social, 28f, 80; spiritual, 48f, 54, 141; subjectivity, 57f, 107, 115

Education as 'provocation', 137f

Evangelist, 21, 136, 162

Examinations in RE, 151f

Experience: and understanding, 130; peak-experiences, 131, 144; religious, 130f, 153f

Faith: as subjective agency, 37f, 62; Christian, 12, 128; in God, 6; religious, 62, 107, 126f, 130, 161f

Freedom: as criterion, 54, 115; of creation, 76; spiritual, 58

God, 6, 8, 13, 25, 26, 39, 41, 56, 59, 108, 118, 120, 127, 128, 163

Hinduism, 161

Human nature, 25f, 32

Imagination, 98f